FUN PAINTING PROJECTS FOR KIDS

60
Activities to
Unleash Your
Inner Artist

FUN PAINTING
PROJECTS
FOR KIDS

LOUISE MCMULLEN
creator of Messy Little Monster®

PAGE STREET
PUBLISHING CO.

Copyright © 2022 Louise McMullen

First published in 2022 by
Page Street Publishing Co.
27 Congress Street, Suite 1511
Salem, MA 01970
www.pagestreetpublishing.com

Distributed by Macmillan, sales in Canada by The Canadian Manda Group.

26 25 24 23 22   1 2 3 4 5

ISBN-13: 978-1-64567-565-5
ISBN-10: 1-64567-565-3

Library of Congress Control Number: 2021950936

Cover and book design by Laura Benton for Page Street Publishing Co.
Photography by Jen Allan Photography

Printed and bound in the United States

DEDICATION

This book is dedicated to Harry, Daisy and Ollie—my three amazing
children who make me smile every day

CONTENTS

INTRODUCTION

I love painting, and because you picked up this book, I'm guessing you do too!

I have included 60 of my favorite painting projects in this collection. From small, detailed paintings you can make indoors to large, abstract outdoor projects, there is something for everyone, whatever your interests, ability or age. My aim with this book is to encourage you to be imaginative and creative and to have fun while painting.

Each project has been tested by creative kids to ensure they are engaging and enjoyable. Younger children will need help with some of the projects, but lots of them are surprisingly easy. Older children may enjoy doing the projects in the book independently, but parental supervision is still advised. It's always fun to work on projects together anyway.

As you start exploring the projects in this book, you'll quickly discover that there are so many fun ways to use paint. Painting is all about expressing yourself, being creative and enjoying the process—and there's no right or wrong way to do it! Look for "Top Tips" included in some of the projects to help you along the way. Use the painting techniques and ideas I've provided as inspiration, but also have fun adapting the projects by changing the colors or themes to suit your interests. Some projects include an "Adapt the Project" section that offers creative variations to try. You'll be amazed by the unique and stunning artwork you'll create!

I have recommended suitable paints in the supply lists to use for each project—either acrylic paints, solid or liquid watercolors, or water-based tempera paints. In many cases, though, the projects will work well with other paint types, so have fun experimenting. For some of the messier projects, washable paints are a good option. Nontoxic paint is also recommended for young children who may put the paints near their mouth.

Most projects in the book call for thick mixed-media paper to paint on. Using good-quality paper can make a big difference in your paintings. Canvases are also great to use for some of the outdoor projects or special paintings. You might want to find a few frames as well to showcase your favorite pieces of artwork.

You can work through the painting projects in order or skip around the book, depending on what catches your eye. Once you've decided where you want to begin, grab your paints and paintbrushes and have fun creating artwork you will be proud of.

For more fun ideas, visit us at www.messylittlemonster.com.

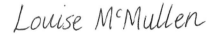

EXPLORING COLOR

Color is such a fun element of art! In this chapter, you'll experiment with mixing up new colors and have fun exploring different color combinations.

Enjoy making your very own color wheel in the shape of a flower (page 12) that not only looks stunning but is also a great tool for understanding the relationship between different colors. Or have fun using various tints and shades to make a beautiful nighttime scene (page 15).

Color choice can be very personal. Do you have a favorite set of colors that you like using to paint with?

FLOWER COLOR WHEEL

Experiment with mixing primary colors (red, blue and yellow) to make secondary colors (orange, green and purple) and make a fun flower-shaped color wheel. Not only is this a great painting project to explore the relationship between colors, but you'll also end up with a beautiful rainbow flower.

SUPPLIES

1 (9-inch [23-cm]) paper plate

Scissors

Red, blue and yellow water-based tempera paints

Paint palette

Paintbrushes

Jar of water, for rinsing brushes

STEP 1: PREPARE YOUR PAPER PLATE

Fold the paper plate into six equal sections. Start by folding the paper plate in half and then folding it into three equal sections. You will end up with a triangle shape.

While the paper plate is folded, hold the pointed end of the triangle shape and cut the top into a petal shape. You will be cutting through all six sections of the paper plate.

When you open up the paper plate, it will look like a flower. Use scissors to neaten up the petals on your flower until you are happy with their shape. You are now ready to turn your flower into a color wheel.

STEP 2: PAINT THE PRIMARY COLORS (RED, BLUE, YELLOW)

Add a squirt of red, blue and yellow paint onto a painting palette, leaving a little room between each color for mixing them together later.

Start by painting one petal red. Use the fold lines in the paper plate to guide you as you paint the whole petal. Leave the next petal white, and then paint the third petal blue. Leave another white petal and then paint a yellow petal. You will end up with alternate petals painted in the three primary colors.

(continued)

TOP TIP

Keep your flower color wheel on hand for future painting projects, as it can help you choose colors and remember how to mix paints.

FLOWER COLOR WHEEL (CONT.)

STEP 3: MIX AND PAINT THE SECONDARY COLORS (GREEN, ORANGE, PURPLE)

Using a paintbrush, mix together a little of the red paint and a little of the blue paint on your palette to create a purple color. Use this purple to paint the petal between the blue and red petals.

Next, mix blue and yellow paint together to make a green color and use it to paint the petal between the yellow and blue petals.

Finally, mix the yellow and red paint together to create an orange color and use it to paint the final petal.

Your flower color wheel is now complete! Hang it up to add a bit of color to your wall, or use it when painting to help you choose your paint colors and remind you how to mix colors.

ADAPT THE PROJECT

You could take this painting project one step further and make a color wheel flower with 12 petals using tertiary colors (red-orange, yellow-orange, yellow-green, blue-green, blue-purple and purple-red) in addition to the primary and secondary colors.

To make a 12-petal flower, fold your paper plate into 12 sections instead of six, hold the pointed end of the folded plate, and cut the top portion into a petal shape.

Paint a petal in each of the primary color paints (red, blue and yellow), leaving 3 white petals between each color. You will be able to add three mixed colors between each primary color. For example, between the red and blue petals you can have blue-purple, purple and purple-red.

NIGHT SKY SILHOUETTE PAINTING
TINTS AND SHADES

Have fun mixing up various tints and shades of blue or purple to paint a beautiful night sky.

By starting with white paint and gradually adding more color to get darker tints, you can create a beautiful night sky with a moon in the center, and it is much easier than you would think! Add a black silhouette on top and you will end up with the most stunning little night sky painting.

SUPPLIES

1 sheet white mixed-media paper

Small bowl, to draw around

Pencil

Scissors

Blue or purple and black and white acrylic paint

Paint palette

Paintbrushes, including a very thin brush

STEP 1: DRAW A CIRCLE

Start by drawing a circle on your paper by tracing around a small bowl. Cut out the circle.

STEP 2: PREPARE YOUR PAINTS

Choose which color you would like to use to create your night sky: blue or purple. Squirt a small amount of your chosen color onto your paint palette. Then squirt a small amount of white on one side of your chosen color and black on the other, leaving room to mix the colors together later.

STEP 3: PAINT YOUR SKY

To paint a night sky, start by painting a white circle in the center of the circle you traced. This will become the moon. Now mix a little of your chosen color (blue or purple) with the white paint on your palette, and use it to paint a circle around the white circle. Mix in a little more of your chosen color and then paint another circle outside the first.

The next circle will be painted using just your original chosen color (blue or purple). Then, for the final circle, add a little black to create a darker shade. Leave your night sky to dry.

Don't worry if your circles of paint blend together a little as you paint them, this just adds to the night sky effect. If you would like the color in your circles to blend more than they have, you can use a slightly damp, clean brush to blend them.

(continued)

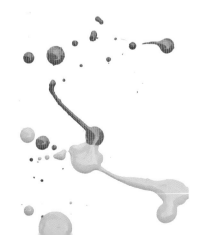

NIGHT SKY SILHOUETTE PAINTING (CONT.)

STEP 4: PAINT YOUR TREE OR BIRD SILHOUETTE

Now it is time to paint your silhouette on top of the night sky using black paint. To paint a tree, start with the tree trunk. Then add branches and small swirls or twigs. To paint birds sitting on a tree branch, start by painting a branch with a few smaller twigs coming off it and then add two birds. Alternatively, come up with your own silhouette design. Maybe you could paint a cat sitting next to a tree or bats flying across the sky.

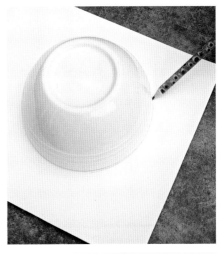

TOP TIP

Draw your silhouette design in pencil first to make sure you are happy with your design before filling it in with black paint.

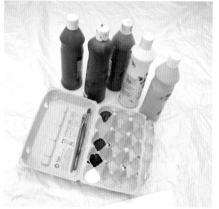
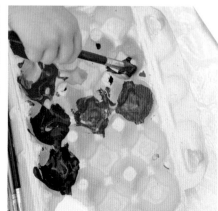

MIX, MIX, MIX!
EXPLORING COLOR MIXING

It is so much fun to mix paints together to see what new colors you can create!
Using just red, blue, yellow, white and black paint, see how many
different colors you can mix up.

For even more fun, have a go at naming the new colors you create! How does
"ocean blue" sound? Or what about "leafy green"?

SUPPLIES

Large egg carton

Red, blue, yellow, white
and black water-based
tempera paints

Paintbrushes

White mixed-media
paper

Pencil

STEP 1: PREPARE YOUR EGG CARTON PAINT PALETTE

Fill the first five sections of the egg carton with red, blue, yellow, white and
black paint. Add one color to each section.

STEP 2: MIX YOUR COLORS

Now it is time to mix up some new colors! Using a paintbrush, scoop up a
little red paint and a little blue paint and mix them in an empty section of the
egg carton. What color have you made? Now add a little white. What color
do you have now?

Continue mixing different combinations of paint together to see what new
colors you can create.

STEP 3: PAINT COLOR SWATCHES

As you mix up different colors, paint small swatches of each one onto a
sheet of paper. Once the paint has dried, see if you can name your colors
using objects that are a similar color as inspiration. You might want to write
the color names next to the swatches with a pencil. A bright yellow could be
"sunshine yellow" or a shade of red could be "rose red." Use your imagination
and see what you can come up with!

COLORFUL HAND
WARM AND COOL COLORS

There is something lovely about creating handprint art, and this colorful hand project doubles as both a keepsake and an eye-catching painting.

Divide your paint colors into warm colors (reds, yellows and oranges) and cool colors (purples, blues and greens) and use them to paint an outline of your hand. See how the warm colors on the hand stand out against the cool colors behind them.

SUPPLIES

1 (5½ x 7–inch [14 x 18-cm]) piece white mixed-media paper

Black permanent marker

Ruler

Watercolor paints

Paintbrush

Jar of water, for rinsing brush

STEP 1: DRAW YOUR HAND OUTLINE AND GRID

Place your hand in the center of the paper and trace around it using a black permanent marker.

Now section off the paper by drawing a grid across it with a ruler. Draw vertical lines roughly ¾ inch (2 cm) apart, and then add horizontal lines roughly ¾ inch (2 cm) apart.

STEP 2: PAINT THE WARM COLORS

All of the squares (or sections of squares) that are within the hand outline are going to be painted in warm colors.

Use a selection of different shades of red, yellow and orange to paint the inner squares.

STEP 3: PAINT THE COOL COLORS

Once the squares painted with warm colors have dried, use cool colors (blues, greens and purples) to paint the squares in the background.

Once you have filled the background, leave your painting to dry.

ADAPT THE PROJECT

Try switching it around and using cool colors for the hand and warm colors for the background.

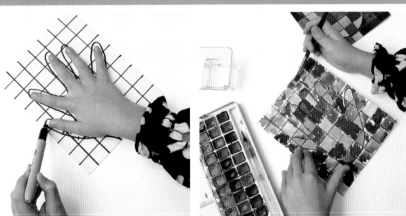

MAKING PRINTS WITH PAINT

Ditch the paintbrushes and have fun making prints using everyday objects. From dipping building blocks in paint to make a skyscraper city (page 41) to making your own creative DIY stamps (page 27), there are so many fun ideas to test out in this chapter.

Some of these projects that use a variety of printing tools—like the Collaborative Flower Painting (page 24), which uses celery, cardboard tubes and even a fork to make prints—are perfect to create with friends as a fun group project!

COLLABORATIVE FLOWER PAINTING

Create a meadow full of flowers by printing with everyday objects. Who knew that a cardboard tube, the end of a bunch of celery, a fork and fingerprints could create such wonderful effects?

This is a fun, collaborative painting project that can be taken in many directions. Use the flower painting ideas as a starting point, but don't worry too much about the order you paint the flowers or about their placement on the page. Just have fun painting alongside your friends or family, adding lots of beautiful flowers to your roll of paper.

SUPPLIES

Large white roll of paper

Pink, purple, yellow (dark and light) and green water-based tempera paints or any colors of your choice

4 plates

Paintbrushes

1 bunch celery

Sharp knife (adults only)

Cardboard tube

Scissors

Fork

STEP 1: PREPARE YOUR WORKSPACE

Roll the paper out and prepare your paints. Add one color to each plate, squirting a thin layer and spreading it out with a paintbrush.

STEP 2: PRINT CELERY ROSES

When you slice the end off a bunch of celery, you are left with the most beautiful pattern that looks just like a rose.

To prepare your rose stamp, you will need to slice about 2¾ or 3 inches (7 or 8 cm) off the end of your celery. This will need to be done with a sharp knife, so ask an adult to help you with this step.

Dip the end of your celery into pink or purple paint and then press it down firmly onto your roll of paper. Carefully lift off the celery and you will be left with a beautiful rose print.

Use your stamp to paint lots of roses across your roll of paper. Once they are dry, paint on stems and leaves using green paint.

STEP 3: PRINT CARDBOARD TUBE SUNFLOWERS

To make a sunflower stamp, cut lots of small 1-inch (2.5-cm) slits into the bottom of a cardboard tube. Then push that end of the cardboard tube down to encourage the small slits to spread out. This will create the petals.

Dip the cardboard tube stamp into yellow paint, and then press the stamp down onto your roll of paper. Make sure all the petals are touching the paper and press firmly. Carefully lift off the carboard tube stamp.

To complete your sunflower, add fingerprint seeds to the center using dark yellow paint. Add a stem and leaves using green paint.

Repeat this process to add lots of sunflowers across your roll of paper.

(continued)

COLLABORATIVE FLOWER PAINTING (CONT.)

STEP 4: PRINT FORK GRASS

A fun way to add grass to your meadow is with a fork. Dip a fork into green paint and then press it firmly onto your roll of paper to create a clump of grass. Repeat across the bottom of the page and fill in the space around your flowers.

STEP 5: FINGERPRINT FLOWERS AND BUTTERFLIES

Complete your flower painting by adding small fingerprint flowers and butterflies in any remaining spaces.

To make a fingerprint flower, print one finger as the center of the flower using a paint color of your choice, and then add 5 fingerprints around the edge of the first with a second color of paint.

To make a fingerprint butterfly, print two fingerprints next to each other at a slight angle in a color of your choice. Then choose a second color and add two fingerprints below the first set. Use a paintbrush to paint the bodies of the butterflies.

ADAPT THE PROJECT

Instead of creating a large-scale collaborative flower painting with your friends, you can also use these techniques to paint on a smaller scale, trying out one flower type at a time.

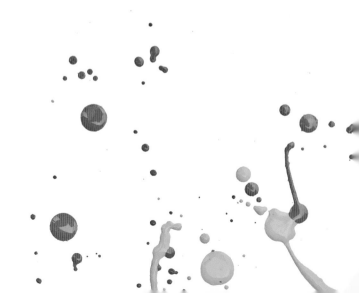

MAKE YOUR OWN STAMPS
POP ART PRINTS

Using just craft foam stickers and cardboard, make your own simple DIY stamps and use them to create some eye-catching pop art.

I'm not sure what I love more about this painting project, the bright contrasting color combinations or the ease with which you can make your own DIY shape stamps.

SUPPLIES

1 heart-shaped craft foam sticker

1 (4½ x 2¼-inch [12 x 6-cm]) piece of cardboard

Scissors

1 star-shaped craft foam sticker

Pencil

Ruler

1 sheet white mixed-media paper

Thin paintbrush

Paint palette

Red, yellow, blue, green, orange and purple acrylic paint or water-based tempera paint

Wipes, for cleaning stamps

Jar of water, for washing brush

STEP 1: MAKE THE SHAPE STAMPS

Stick the foam heart sticker onto the cardboard and then cut the cardboard around the sticker into a 2¼ x 2¼-inch (6 x 6-cm) square. Repeat with the star sticker.

STEP 2: DRAW A GRID

Using a pencil and ruler, draw a 3 x 2 grid on the paper. Each grid square needs to be 2½ x 2½ inches (6.5 x 6.5 cm).

STEP 3: PRINT STAR AND HEART SHAPES

Paint your star stamp with green paint. Then hold the painted stamp above the first grid square and press it down firmly. Carefully lift up the stamp to reveal your star print. Clean the stamp in between each color using a wipe.

Now repeat this process in the next square to print an orange heart followed by a purple star. In the grid squares on the bottom row, print a yellow heart, red star and blue heart. Allow it to dry.

(continued)

TOP TIP

If you don't have foam stickers or you want to experiment with different shapes, you can cut custom shapes from craft foam and then glue them to your cardboard.

MAKE YOUR OWN STAMPS (CONT.)

STEP 4: PAINT THE BACKGROUND

Carefully paint the background of each square using contrasting colors. Paint the background of the green star in red, the background of the orange heart in blue, the background of the purple star in yellow, the background of the yellow heart in purple, the background of the red star in green and the background of the blue heart in orange. Your pop art project is now complete!

ADAPT THE PROJECT

A black-and-white version of this pop art project could look really striking!

BLACK-AND-WHITE SYMMETRY BUGS

Black-and-white prints always look so striking! These symmetry bug prints couldn't be simpler, but they are so much fun to make that you won't be able to stop.

SUPPLIES

1 sheet white paper

Black water-based tempera paint

Paint palette

Thin paintbrush

Pencil (optional)

STEP 1: PAINT HALF A BUG

Fold a piece of paper in half and then open it up. Using black paint and a thin paintbrush, paint a picture of half a bug on one side of the paper up to the fold line. You might find it easier to paint your bug if you draw the picture in pencil first. Look at images of real bugs to help you.

STEP 2: MAKE A PRINT

Make sure the paint is still wet. If it isn't, paint back over the lines. Then fold the paper in half along the fold line you created in step 1.

Press firmly and then carefully open up the paper to reveal a full print of your painted bug. The reveal is the best part! There is no way you will want to stop at making just one bug print, so see how many different bugs you can make.

ADAPT THE PROJECT

Black-and-white prints look great, but if you prefer using color, you can paint in the black outlines once they have dried.

BUBBLE WRAP PAINTING
HOT AIR BALLOON

Making bubble wrap prints is both easy and fun. Whether you want to explore the interesting patterns that you can make with this printing technique or follow the directions for making a hot air balloon picture, you are sure to have fun!

SUPPLIES

Thick paintbrush

Paint palette

Light blue, dark blue, yellow, orange, gray, green, red and purple water-based tempera paints

4 sheets white mixed-media paper

Scissors

Bubble wrap

Tape

Wipes, for cleaning bubble wrap

White glue

ADAPT THE PROJECT

What other pictures can you create by cutting shapes from your bubble wrap prints?

STEP 1: MAKE BUBBLE WRAP PRINTS

Paint a piece of paper light blue and another piece of paper yellow and allow them to dry.

Cut a piece of bubble wrap slightly larger than your paper and tape the bubble wrap to the table. Paint the bubble wrap dark blue with a thick paintbrush, being sure to cover all the bubbles evenly. While the bubble wrap is still wet, place your light blue painted paper on top of it and press down firmly. Lift up the paper to reveal your bubble wrap print. This is your sky.

Now clean your bubble wrap or cut a fresh piece and paint it orange. Place the yellow painted paper on top and press it down. Lift the paper to reveal your print. This paper will be for your basket.

You are now going to make your rainbow bubble wrap print that will be for the balloon. Paint stripes in green, yellow, orange, red and purple across a clean piece of bubble wrap and then press a piece of white paper on top. Peel it back to reveal your print.

The last printed paper you need to make is for the clouds. Paint a piece of bubble wrap in gray, press a piece of white paper on top and then peel it off.

Mix things up a little if you like and use bubble wrap with different-sized bubbles to make your prints.

STEP 2: CUT OUT BUBBLE WRAP PRINTED PAPER

Once your bubble wrap prints are dry, cut them into shapes to create your picture. To make a hot air balloon, draw around a mug to create a circle on your rainbow print and then cut it out. Next, draw and cut out your basket shape—including the ropes—from the orange print and then finally cut three cloud shapes from the gray print.

STEP 3: MAKE YOUR HOT AIR BALLOON PICTURE

Your blue bubble wrap print is your sky. Lay the cutout clouds and hot air balloon on the sky to create your hot air balloon picture. When you are happy with their position, glue them in place.

TOTALLY UNIQUE MONOPRINTS

Make a one-of-a-kind print that is as unique as you are with this fun monoprint technique. No two prints will be the same, which gives you the opportunity to have fun experimenting with different colors and designs.

SUPPLIES

Water-based tempera paints in any colors of your choice

Paint pot

Foam paintbrush or small foam roller

9 x 13-inch (23 x 33-cm) baking dish with a smooth bottom or any flat glass surface

Cotton swabs (optional)

Several sheets white paper

Wipes, for cleaning baking dish

STEP 1: DRAW YOUR DESIGN IN A THIN LAYER OF PAINT

Squirt some paint into a paint pot. Using a foam paintbrush or roller, apply a thin layer of paint to the bottom side of the baking dish. You can use one color or a combination of colors.

Using a cotton swab or your finger, if you prefer, draw a design in the thin layer of paint. Any lines you draw will appear white in your final print. Keep your designs simple. Items such as leaves, flowers, hearts, stars and so on work well, as do patterns, or scribbles for younger children.

STEP 2: LAY PAPER OVER YOUR DESIGN

When you are happy with your design, carefully lay a piece of paper on the top of the paint and press it down firmly with your hands. Make sure all areas of the paper have been pressed evenly.

STEP 3: REVEAL YOUR PRINT

Now for the best part! It is time to reveal your print. Carefully peel the paper away from the baking dish to see your completed monoprint.

You won't want to make just one print—this process is surprisingly addictive. Just add more paint to the baking dish and you are ready to go again. If you are changing paint colors, you may want to wipe down the baking dish in between prints so you don't get muddy colors.

SHAVING CREAM AND PAINT MARBLING

You won't be able to get enough of this cool marbling project! Making marbled paper using this technique is such a fun sensory experience, and the final prints look so pretty.

SUPPLIES

Shaving cream

Small tray

Water-based tempera paints in any colors of your choice

Skewer or paintbrush

Several (4 x 6–inch [10 x 15–cm]) pieces white mixed-media paper

Ruler

TOP TIP

Turn your marbled prints into greeting cards or cut them up to make bookmarks.

STEP 1: CREATE YOUR PATTERN IN SHAVING CREAM

Squirt a thin layer of shaving cream into your tray and spread it out. Then squirt tempera paint in a variety of colors on top of the shaving cream. Using a skewer or the end of a paintbrush, swirl the colors around to make swirly patterns in the shaving cream.

STEP 2: TAKE A PRINT OF THE PATTERN

Lay a piece of paper on top of the shaving cream and pat it down gently so that the shaving cream and paint are touching the front of the paper all over. Carefully remove the paper and lay it down on a protected surface. Use a ruler to scrape off the shaving foam and reveal a pretty marbled pattern.

You won't be able to stop at making just one print! Using the shaving cream and paint you have already added, you should be able to take one or two more prints. If you want to make more, keep adding more shaving cream and paint to your tray as needed.

SPONGE PAINTING
BUTTERFLIES

Make a symmetrical butterfly using a simple stamp made from a sponge. When you add an elastic band to the center of a sponge it creates the perfect butterfly shape for making beautiful prints.

SUPPLIES

Elastic band

Small rectangular sponge

Thick paintbrushes

Paint palette

Pink, yellow and purple water-based tempera paints or any colors of your choice

Several sheets white mixed-media paper

Acrylic paint pen or marker in purple or any color of your choice

STEP 1: MAKE A BUTTERFLY STAMP

Wrap an elastic band around the center of a sponge two or three times to create a butterfly shape.

Paint the outer edge of both butterfly wings with a strip of yellow paint and then paint the rest of the sponge pink. Be generous with the amount of paint you use. Add a few lines of purple paint toward the center of the butterfly. Now fold the sponge stamp in half to make sure both sides are the same.

Press your butterfly stamp onto a piece of paper firmly and then carefully lift it off.

Repeat the process to add more butterflies to your paper, and then allow your prints to dry.

STEP 2: ADD BUTTERFLY DETAILS

Use a purple paint pen or marker to draw the center of the butterfly between the wings. Add a few dots to the butterfly's wings with your paint pen for added interest, trying to keep them symmetrical if you can.

ADAPT THE PROJECT

Try out different color combinations and experiment with painting different patterns on your butterfly stamp. Why not make a whole sky full of sponge-painted butterflies?

SKYSCRAPER CITY
PRINTING WITH BUILDING BLOCKS

Create your own amazing skyscraper city! Printing with building blocks dipped into paint creates a really cool effect that you can use to design a city full of skyscrapers. Making white prints on a black background results in buildings that look really striking.

SUPPLIES

Building blocks in a variety of shapes and sizes

White water-based tempera paint

Plate or paint palette

Paintbrush

1 large sheet black paper

STEP 1: PREPARE YOUR STAMPS

To make the building block pieces easy to print with, create a small handle on each block by adding a smaller block on top of it.

Squirt a thin layer of white paint onto a plate or paint palette, spreading it out using a paintbrush.

STEP 2: PRINT WITH BUILDING BLOCKS

Dip the building blocks into the white paint and then press them firmly onto the black paper.

Keep adding more prints next to each other to make your skyscrapers. I would suggest starting at the bottom left-hand corner of your paper and working your way across.

You can be as imaginative as you like! What would you like to include in your skyscraper city?

ADAPT THE PROJECT

What else could you make with building blocks prints? A robot? Or maybe a rocket?

SPECIAL EFFECT PAINTING

There are so many fun ways to create cool effects with paint. In this chapter you'll explore some fun painting techniques that will make you say WOW!

From experimenting with different resist techniques, like oil pastel resist, to making colorful popsicles (page 48), blowing paint with a straw to create a crazy new hairstyle (page 71) or even painting with ice (page 79), there are sure to be a few painting techniques you have never tried.

Not only can you use the techniques in this chapter to make the corresponding paintings, but you can also use them to experiment and come up with your own projects.

DRIP DROP RAIN PAINTING

Can you resist jumping in puddles and dancing in the rain? This painting project is perfect for anyone who loves the rain. It involves creating a rainy scene using a fun drip painting technique. What makes it even more exciting is that after creating your rainy scene, you can add yourself in the painting.

This painting technique can get messy, as some paint will drip off the bottom of your canvas. For that reason, I would suggest doing it outdoors or on a protected floor.

SUPPLIES

1 canvas or sheet mixed-media paper attached to a clipboard

Easel or a place to prop up your canvas

Light blue, dark blue and purple liquid acrylic paint or liquid watercolors

3 paint pots

3 pipettes

Paintbrush

Camera

Printer

White printer paper

White glue

ADAPT THE PROJECT

If you don't have a photograph, you could draw or paint a picture of someone holding an umbrella to add to your painting.

STEP 1: PAINT THE RAIN

Prop your canvas up on an easel or at an angle against a wall. Then prepare the light blue, dark blue and purple liquid acrylic paints by pouring small amounts of each color into paint pots. You will need one pipette for each color.

Using a pipette, drip one color at a time from the top of your canvas and watch as it dribbles down the front like rain. Repeat using all the colors until your canvas is filled with rain. Once you are happy with the coverage, lay your canvas flat to dry.

Try to prevent the drips from touching each other so the colors won't merge together. Once your painting has dried, if you feel your painting needs it, you can add more drips of blue paint.

STEP 2: PAINT A PUDDLE

Using a paintbrush and blue paint, paint a puddle shape near the bottom of your canvas. Flick a little color around the puddle to create a splash effect.

STEP 3: ADD A PHOTO

To make your rain painting really personal, add a black and white photograph of yourself with an umbrella and rain boots. Have fun trying out different poses and then print your favorite one. Cut out the photograph and glue it onto the canvas just above the puddle. Your rain painting is now ready to hang with pride!

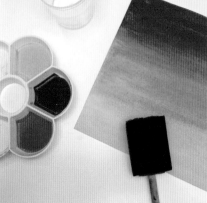

DINOSAUR SHADOW PAINTING

Have fun exploring the wet-on-wet watercolor technique to create a beautiful sunset sky. The color blends that appear when you apply watercolors to a wet page are beautiful. But don't stop there! Once your night sky has dried, have fun painting a dinosaur silhouette on top with black paint. If you don't know how to draw dinosaurs, don't worry. I have the perfect solution: shadow tracing!

SUPPLIES

1 sheet white mixed-media paper

Jar of water, for making wash and rinsing brush

Thick paintbrush

Red, orange and yellow liquid watercolors

A bright light

Toy dinosaur figures

Pencil

Black acrylic paint

STEP 1: PAINT A NIGHT SKY

Start by painting your paper with water, filling the whole page. The paper should feel damp, but not completely soaked. Using a thick paintbrush, paint a few rows of yellow paint across the top of the paper. Then continue painting across the paper with orange paint, finally ending with red paint. Make sure the paper is completely covered, going back to add extra paint to any areas you feel need it.

STEP 2: TRACE A DINOSAUR

Once your night sky has dried, draw a dinosaur on top. A perfect way to do this is to draw around the shadow of a toy dinosaur.

Lay your night sky painting on a flat surface with a strong light source behind it. You can either use a lamp or take your project outdoors on a sunny day.

Move the toy dinosaur and your piece of paper around until you are happy with the shadow the toy is casting on the paper. Trace around the shadow with a pencil.

STEP 3: PAINT THE DINOSAUR

Complete your dinosaur silhouette by painting the dinosaur outline you drew with black acrylic paint. You may also want to add some grass along the bottom of your paper, or even some trees.

ADAPT THE PROJECT

This painting project would work really well using jungle animals for the silhouettes. Instead of tracing dinosaur toys, find some jungle animals to trace instead.

OIL PASTEL RESIST
POPSICLE CRAFT

Oil pastels are brilliant for keeping watercolor paint where you want it! They resist watercolors because oil and water don't mix. This means that oil pastels can be used as a watercolor barrier. In this painting project, we are using the oil pastel resist technique to paint some yummy-looking popsicles!

SUPPLIES

Pencil

1 sheet white mixed-media paper

Scissors

Oil pastels in bright colors

Liquid or solid watercolors in bright colors

Paintbrushes

Glue or tape

Craft sticks (one for each popsicle)

Jar of water, for rinsing brushes

STEP 1: DRAW PATTERNS WITH OIL PASTELS

Draw popsicle shapes onto your paper and then cut them out. If you are making lots of popsicles, I suggest drawing one popsicle shape, cutting it out and then using it as a template to draw the rest.

Use oil pastels to draw various patterns and shapes on your popsicles, pressing the oil pastels firmly against the paper. You can be creative here—there is no right or wrong way to do this. You can section areas off by drawing lines from one side of the popsicle shape to the other, as well as drawing smaller lines and patterns.

STEP 2: PAINT WITH WATERCOLOR PAINT

Now to add some color. Use watercolor paints to paint the different sections of your popsicles. The marks you have made using oil pastels will still show even if you paint over them, but if you want to have sections painted in different colors, be careful not to paint outside the oil pastel lines. Have fun using lots of bright colors to make your popsicles look good enough to eat.

STEP 3: ADD A POPSICLE STICK

Once the paint has dried, turn your paintings over and glue or tape a popsicle stick to the back. Your popsicle craft is now complete.

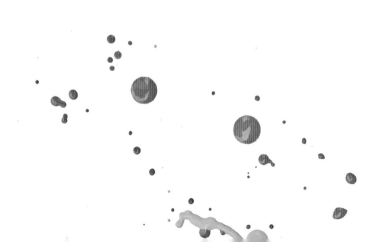

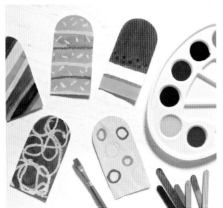

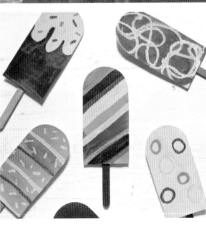

SECRET MOTIVATIONAL MESSAGES

Everyone loves a bit of positivity, and these motivational messages will definitely make someone smile. Write positive messages to friends and family using a white oil pastel on white paper. The oil pastel message will be almost invisible at first, but your family and friends just need to apply watercolor paint to the paper to reveal your secret message. But don't miss out on all the positivity—let them do one for you too!

SUPPLIES

Several (4 x 6–inch [10 x 15–cm]) pieces white mixed-media paper

White oil pastel

Liquid or solid watercolor paint in any color of your choice

Paint palette

Paintbrush

Jar of water, for rinsing brush

STEP 1: WRITE YOUR MOTIVATIONAL MESSAGE

Think about who you will be giving your secret message to and think of a motivational message for them. Here are some examples:

You are amazing

You are awesome

You're unique

Follow your heart

Dream big

Be happy

Be brave

Be amazing today

Believe in yourself

Anything is possible

You've got this

You make me happy

Make it count

Smile

Write your message on your paper using a white oil pastel. As you write the message it can be hard to see what you have already written, so I suggest writing the full message in one go without stopping.

STEP 2: REVEAL YOUR MESSAGE

Now it is time to give your motivational message to someone special. Tell them to reveal their message by painting the piece of paper using watercolor paint.

Not only will this activity make someone smile, but these messages are great to display around the house.

SCRATCH ART
MINI SCENES

Making your own scratch art papers is surprisingly easy. Using just oil pastels, paint and dish soap, you can make them in no time. The big question is what mini scene will you scratch away?

SUPPLIES

Oil pastels in bright colors

Several (4 x 6-inch [10 x 15-cm]) pieces white mixed-media paper

Paint pot

Black acrylic paint

Dish soap

Paintbrush

Toothpicks

STEP 1: PREPARE THE SCRATCH ART PAPER

Use oil pastels to fill the paper with color. There should be no white left. I suggest applying thick stripes of each color diagonally across your paper, although any design will work just so long as the paper is completely full of color.

STEP 2: PAINT THE SCRATCH ART PAPER

Mix together a generous squirt of black acrylic paint with two or three drops of dish soap. Paint over the entire piece of paper using the paint and dish soap mixture. Then allow the paint to fully dry. One coat of paint should be enough, but if you can still see the oil pastel colors showing through, add a second coat of paint.

STEP 3: SCRATCH THE PAINT AWAY

Now for the fun part! Use a toothpick to scratch away the paint to reveal the colors underneath. You can use the toothpick to draw anything you like, but creating a mini scene is a lot of fun. Maybe scratch away a city at night or a rocket surrounded by planets and stars?

As you scratch away more lines, you'll reveal all the different colors you added under the black paint. The rainbow colors look really striking against the black background.

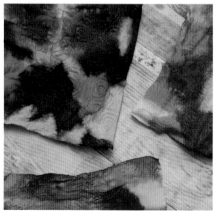

PAPER TOWEL ART

Turn paper towels into bright and colorful pieces of art! The process of dropping color onto paper towels and watching it spread is so exciting, especially as the colors start to merge together. This technique creates beautiful artwork, and the results are unique every time. You can also turn your paper towel art into the most adorable, but easy, butterfly craft!

This painting technique can get messy, as the paint will soak through the paper towel onto whatever surface is underneath. I suggest protecting your workspace with a waterproof cloth. You could also lay down newspaper for extra protection or paint on a tray.

SUPPLIES

Paper towels

Red, yellow, orange, green, blue and purple liquid watercolors or diluted food coloring

Pipettes or paintbrushes

Paint palette

Waterproof cloth, newspaper or tray to protect workspace

Clothespins (optional)

Pipe cleaners (optional)

STEP 1: DRIP PAINT ONTO A PAPER TOWEL

Lay a paper towel out flat on your work surface and choose your paint colors. You can use all the colors in the supply list or just a few. Using all the colors is a good idea if you would like to explore what happens as the different colors mix.

Once you have chosen your colors, use a pipette or paintbrush to carefully drop a little paint onto the paper towel. Repeat using all your chosen colors and watch as the paint spreads and the colors merge. Experiment with using small drops of paint and larger drops of paint.

When the paper towel is full of color, allow it to dry by placing it on top of a second paper towel. The color will seep through the first paper towel to the paper towel underneath, leaving you with two pieces of paper towel art!

STEP 2: MAKE A BUTTERFLY (OPTIONAL)

While the paper towel art looks beautiful on its own, it can be fun to use your artwork to make something else—in this case, a butterfly.

To make a paper towel butterfly, carefully scrunch up the dry paper towel down the center. This will create two wing shapes with a pinched part in the center. Clamp a clothespin to the pinched part to hold it in place.

If you want to add antennae, fold a 2¾-inch (7-cm) piece of pipe cleaner in half and clamp it into the clothespin.

COFFEE PAINTING
MAKE A TREASURE MAP

Ahoy there! Prepare yourself for making your own authentic-looking treasure map using coffee paint. The coffee paint will give your ancient treasure map a perfect aged look. Have fun using your imagination as you dream up the details of your pirate treasure map. Only your imagination is the limit to what can be included—just don't forget that X marks the spot!

Why not use your treasure map as a prompt for starting your own pirate adventure!

SUPPLIES

Instant or regular coffee

Hot water

3 mugs

Teaspoon

Thick paintbrush

1 sheet white mixed-media paper

Thin paintbrush

Ribbon (optional)

STEP 1: MIX UP YOUR COFFEE PAINT

You will need three shades of coffee paint to make your treasure map. To make coffee paint, simply add coffee and hot water to a mug and mix them together. Follow the ratios below to make each of the three shades.

- **Lightest shade:** Mix 1 heaping teaspoon of coffee with 1 cup (240 ml) of hot water

- **Medium shade:** Mix 1 heaping teaspoon of coffee with ¼ cup (60 ml) of hot water

- **Darkest shade:** Mix 1 heaping teaspoon of coffee with 1 teaspoon of hot water

STEP 2: PAINT THE SEA

Apply the lightest shade of coffee paint to your piece of paper. This will become the sea. I recommend using a thick paintbrush to paint this area. Try not to get your paper too wet, or it will take a long time to dry.

STEP 3: PAINT THE LAND

Once the sea has dried, use the medium shade of coffee paint to create the land. Paint the outline of land in the center of your paper and think carefully about the shape you would like it to be. Once you are happy with your outline, fill it in with the medium shade of coffee paint. You can also use your medium shade of coffee paint to add a few waves in your sea. Allow it to dry.

STEP 4: PAINT THE DETAILS

Make sure your treasure map is completely dry before beginning this step. You are now going to use your darkest shade of coffee paint and a thin paintbrush to add all the details.

On the land you could paint trees, mountains, swamps, rocks and a skull and crossbones, and in the sea you could add sharks and a pirate ship. Use your imagination, and add all the things that you think are important to have on a treasure map. And don't forget—X marks the spot!

STEP 5: ADD A RIBBON (OPTIONAL)

Once your treasure map has dried, roll it up into a scroll and tie a piece of ribbon around it. You are now ready to head off on a pirate adventure!

TOP TIP

Design your treasure map on a spare piece of paper before you start painting.

RAISED SALT PAINTING

Who doesn't love raised salt painting? It is such a cool painting technique, and the results are beautiful. Try out various designs and be mesmerized as you watch the paint slowly travel along the salt.

SUPPLIES

1 sheet white mixed-media paper

Small (4-ounce [118-ml]) bottle white glue with nozzle

Table salt

Paintbrushes

Liquid watercolors in bright colors

Paint palette

Jar of water, for rinsing brushes

STEP 1: CREATE YOUR DESIGN USING GLUE

Draw a design on your paper using the bottle of glue. To create thin, steady lines of glue, you need to squeeze the bottle quite hard and move it at a steady pace. You might want to practice a little on a spare piece of paper first.

When deciding what to draw with your glue, simple shapes work best. Drawing a spider's web to fill with bright colors can look really cool.

To create a spider's web, start by drawing several lines that intersect at the center of your paper, creating a star shape. Then add smaller lines between them to create a web shape.

Other fun design ideas you could try are a heart shape, a large snowflake, fireworks, your name or even a scribble. Just think big and bold when you are choosing your designs, as it is hard to add small details with the glue.

STEP 2: ADD SALT

Once you have finished your glue picture, sprinkle table salt over your entire design. Be generous with the salt and ensure all the glue is completely covered. Then tap off any extra salt and leave the salt and glue to dry. Pour extra salt off into a tray so it can be used for future projects.

STEP 3: PAINTING TIME!

Now it is time to add some color. Dip a paintbrush into some watercolor paint and then lightly touch the salt with it. Watch as the color from your paintbrush spreads across the salt like magic. Repeat using various colors until all your lines of salt are covered in bright colors. Then allow the salt painting to dry overnight.

ADAPT THE PROJECT

Try salt painting on black paper. This works especially well if you are doing a firework or star design, as the black background will look like the night sky.

SMUSH PAINTING
GALAXY ART

Use your hands to smush paint and make this awesome galaxy art. The best bit is that you don't even need to get your hands messy! With just a bit of plastic wrap, you can smush paint all day long if you like, and your hands will stay clean. Add a few splats of white paint to your smush painting, and your galaxy art will look so awesome that everyone will want one!

SUPPLIES

Black, dark blue, light blue, purple, pink and white water-based tempera paints

1 canvas in any size of your choice

Plastic wrap

Paintbrush

ADAPT THE PROJECT

Try this technique using different color combinations to make a completely different set of smush art.

STEP 1: PREPARE YOUR CANVAS

Squirt lots of blobs of black paint directly onto your canvas. Don't hold back on the amount of paint you are using; you will need more than you think!

Squirt some smaller blobs of dark blue, light blue, pink and purple paint, and then finally drizzle over a little extra black paint.

Cut a piece of plastic that is slightly larger than your canvas and place it on top of your paint. If you have a really large canvas, you may need more than one piece of plastic wrap. Carefully fold the plastic wrap around the edges of your canvas.

STEP 2: SMUSH THE PAINT

Using your hands, smush the paint under the plastic wrap and watch how the colors merge into each other and overlap.

You can use your full hand or your fingertips to squash the paint and squish it around.

Keep going until there is no white left on the canvas and all the colors have merged together.

Now carefully peel back the plastic wrap to reveal your galaxy painting.

STEP 3: FLICK WHITE PAINT

To finish it off, dip a paintbrush into white paint and use it to flick white paint across your painting. You may like to add some flicks of pink paint too.

Allow it to dry flat. Since a lot of paint is used to create this galaxy art, it will take several days to dry.

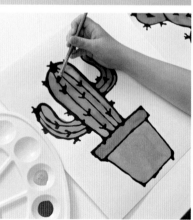

BLACK GLUE RESIST
CACTUS PAINTING

Black glue resists watercolors brilliantly, creating bold outlines. Use this easy resist technique to create some cool cactuses.

Small (4-ounce [118-ml]) bottle white glue with nozzle

Black acrylic paint

Paintbrushes

1 sheet white mixed-media paper

Pencil (optional)

Green, orange and yellow liquid watercolors

Paint palette

Jar of water, for rinsing brushes

STEP 1: MAKE YOUR BLACK GLUE

Pour out about 25 percent of the white glue from the bottle, and store it somewhere for future use. Then fill the space left in the bottle with black acrylic paint. Shake it well and then mix it using the end of a paintbrush. Replace the nozzle on the glue bottle, and your black glue is ready to use. You can also use this black glue to make pictures like the Take a Line for a Walk painting on page 142.

STEP 2: DRAW YOUR CACTUS

Now it is time to draw a picture of a cactus in a pot on your paper using the black glue. You may want to practice squeezing the glue from the bottle first so you can get used to the pressure needed and flow before you start your picture. It may also help to draw your cactus picture in pencil first.

Carefully squeeze the glue bottle and draw your cactus shape using a thin black line of glue. If you end up with a few blobby areas, don't worry—that just adds to the effect. Once you have drawn the outline of your cactus and the pot, add any details you would like to include like small spines. Then allow the black glue to dry completely.

STEP 3: PAINT TIME!

Once the glue has dried, it is time to paint it using the watercolors. Water the paints down slightly on your palette if you wish, and then paint the cactus green and the pot orange or yellow. The black glue will resist the paint, making it easier to stay within the lines.

ADAPT THE PROJECT

This painting technique can be used for so many themes. Once you have made a cactus picture, try drawing other subjects with black glue.

PAINT BLOB CHALLENGE

Here is a fun little challenge for you: Exercise your imagination and turn blobs of paint into pictures. Add blobs of paint in different colors and shapes to a piece of paper, then when they are dry, use your imagination to turn the paint blobs into drawings. What will you turn your blobs into?

SUPPLIES

Paintbrush

Liquid watercolors or any other paint in any colors of your choice

1 sheet white mixed-media paper

Jar of water, for washing brush

Fine tip black marker

STEP 1: PAINT BLOBS

Paint a variety of random blobs on the paper. Take your time and think about the shapes and colors you would like to use. You can keep all the blobs as circles and ovals or make more unusual shapes if you prefer. Don't think about what they will be turned into yet—save that for later!

Try to leave a gap between each of the blobs so there is room to add drawings later.

STEP 2: TURN THE PAINT BLOBS INTO PICTURES

Once the paint blobs have dried, take a look at them and think about what they remind you of. Maybe an oval orange blob looks a little like a fish, or a round green blob looks like the top of a tree.

Use a fine tip black marker to transform your paint blobs into the objects that you decide they most look like. Use the marker to add details both on and around the paint blob.

This challenge is about being creative and having fun doodling. In addition to turning blobs into everyday objects, you could use the paint blobs as a starting point for creating your own unique and silly characters or creatures. Only your imagination is the limit to what you can design.

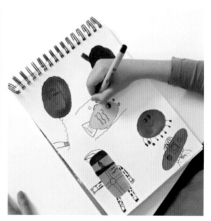

WATERCOLOR AND SALT UNDERWATER WORLD

Put your imagination and creative skills to the test as you paint your own underwater world full of fish, sea creatures and underwater plants. You can even add mermaids and pirate chests if you wish!

To add extra interest, use the watercolor salt technique to produce a really cool and unique background. You can't control exactly how your painting will look when using this technique, and it is exciting to see how it turns out.

SUPPLIES

2 sheets white mixed-media paper

Paintbrush

Paint palette

Jar of water, for washing brush

Blue liquid watercolor paint

Sea salt

Solid watercolor paints in any colors of your choice

Scissors

White glue

STEP 1: CREATE YOUR BACKGROUND

Paint one sheet of paper completely blue using liquid watercolor paint. While the paint is still wet, sprinkle a pinch or two of sea salt across your paper and then allow the painting to dry.

Watch as the salt pushes the color away, creating lighter areas surrounded by darker ones. This effect happens quite quickly.

When the paint has completely dried, lightly brush the salt away. Don't be tempted to brush the salt away before it is completely dry, or it will spoil the effect.

STEP 2: PAINT SEA CREATURES

On the second sheet of paper, paint a collection of fish, sea creatures and underwater plants with watercolor paints. Look at pictures of sea creatures for reference. You might like to draw your pictures before painting them. Allow your sea creatures to dry.

STEP 3: GLUE SEA CREATURES TO YOUR BACKDROP

Cut out your watercolor sea creatures and lay them on your sea background. When you are happy with your composition, glue the sea creatures in place. Your underwater world is now complete.

SCRAPE PAINTING
MINI PICTURES

Scrape painting is such an easy painting technique, but the results look surprisingly complex. By scraping dots of paint across a piece of paper, you can easily create colorful abstract art that will look amazing on display.

SUPPLIES

1 sheet white mixed-media paper

Masking tape

Red, yellow, orange, pink, green, blue and purple acrylic paints or any colors of your choice

Thick piece poster board with straight edge

Small frames (optional)

STEP 1: ADD DROPS OF PAINT

Secure a sheet of paper to your work surface using tape across the top and bottom of the paper. Make sure the paper doesn't move, as you want it to stay still when you scrape it.

Carefully squeeze small drops of paint in your chosen colors straight from the paint bottles. Add them in a random pattern across the page, making sure you have several drops near the top.

If you don't want any colors mixing, just add colors across the top of your paper.

STEP 2: SCRAPE THE PAINT

Take a piece of poster board with a straight edge that is the size of your piece of paper and use it to scrape the paint from one side of your paper to the other. Use firm pressure as you drag the paint, and keep going until you are past the end of the paper.

STEP 3: CUT YOUR SCRAPE PAINTING INTO MINI PICTURES (OPTIONAL)

Once your painting has dried, you might decide you would like to display it as is, but there is something lovely about creating mini pictures.

To make mini pictures, choose your favorite sections of your scrape painting and cut them to the size of your small frames. Add your artwork to the frames and find a special spot to display them.

ADAPT THE PROJECT

Use your scrape paintings to make greeting cards or bookmarks.

BLOW PAINTING
CRAZY HAIR DAY

Give yourself a new crazy hairstyle with this fun blow-painting project. Use a photograph of your face or draw a picture of your face, the choice is yours. You won't be able to stop giggling as you blow paint in all directions to give yourself some crazy rainbow hair.

SUPPLIES

Camera

White printer paper

Printer

Scissors

White glue

1 sheet white mixed-media paper

Pipettes

Liquid acrylic paints or liquid watercolors in rainbow colors

Drinking straw

ADAPT THE PROJECT

This blow-painting technique can be used for so many fun projects. Try making blow-paint monsters, complete with googly eyes, or draw a lion's face and use the blow-painting technique to make its mane.

STEP 1: TAKE A PHOTO

Ask somebody to take a photograph of you that includes your head and shoulders. Print the photograph out in black and white, and then cut it out so there is no background. Glue the cutout photograph onto the mixed-media paper, making sure you leave lots of room at the top.

This painting project is more fun if you can use a photograph of your face, but if you don't have one, you can draw a picture of your face instead.

STEP 2: ADD DROPLETS OF PAINT

Using a pipette, squirt a small droplet of each color of paint along the top of the photograph of your face. Start above the ear on the left with green paint, followed by blue, then purple, red, orange and finally yellow. Space the drops out so you end up with the last drop by the right ear.

You can also mix up the order of the colors if you would prefer, so you have various different colors all over your head.

STEP 3: BLOW!

Now for the really fun part! Grab your straw and, with your photograph facing you, carefully blow the droplets of paint upward, one at a time, and outward, away from the face. As you blow the paint, it will create crazy lines that wiggle in all directions.

Make sure you only blow through the straw, being careful not to suck up the paint instead! Younger children may need an adult to help them direct the straw before they blow the paint.

Once you have blown all the droplets of paint, you can add more paint if you would like a fuller crazy hairstyle.

PUFFY PAINT DONUTS

Have you ever made puffy paint? Mixing up a batch is really easy, and its puffy texture is so much fun to paint with.

Puffy paint is the perfect paint recipe for making the icing on pretend donuts, as the paint looks good enough to eat, but it definitely IS NOT edible, so don't be tempted to actually try eating it! What's more, there is glue in the paint, so you can add all kinds of pretend sprinkles to your donuts without having to individually glue them into place.

Making puffy paint donuts is such a fun sensory experience, and once the puffy paint icing on your cardboard donuts has dried, it will have a soft and foamy feel. How cool is that?

SUPPLIES

1 cup (240 ml) shaving cream (for each color)

1 cup (240 ml) white glue (for each color)

Small bowls (one for each color)

Red liquid watercolor paint or food coloring and any other colors of your choice

Paintbrushes

Scissors

Cardboard

Small bowl

Pencil

Sprinkles (sequins, pom-poms, gems, etc.)

STEP 1: MAKE YOUR PUFFY PAINT

To make pink puffy paint, combine the shaving cream and white glue in a small bowl. Then add 5 to 10 drops of red liquid watercolor paint or food coloring and mix everything together using a paintbrush. If you would like your pink to look a little darker, add more drops of red coloring, but bear in mind that the puffy paint will get a little darker as it dries. Repeat for any additional colors you would like to use and set aside for later.

STEP 2: PREPARE YOUR DONUTS

Cut your cardboard into donut shapes. Trace around the outside of a small bowl to create a circle and cut it out. Then draw a smaller circle inside and cut it out. Once you have cut out one donut, use it as a template to make any others. I suggest making lots, as this activity is addictive and you will want to make more pretend donuts than you think!

STEP 3: MAKE YOUR DONUTS

Now for the fun part! Set up your workspace with your cardboard donuts, puffy paint and a selection of "sprinkles." You can use anything you have available for sprinkles: sequins, gems, small pom-poms and whatever else you think will look good on your donuts.

Then use a large paintbrush to scoop your puffy paint onto your donut. You will want to use lots of paint, so it looks really puffy. Once you are happy with your coverage of puffy paint, it is time to add your sprinkles. The puffy paint will keep the sprinkles in place, so there is no need to add any extra glue. Once you have added enough sprinkles, let your puffy paint donuts dry.

SPIN ART BIRDS

Salad spinners aren't just for drying your lettuce; they are also the perfect tool for spinning paint and creating some wonderful effects. Watching paint spin inside a salad spinner is lots of fun, but the best bit is lifting the lid at the end to see what your final painting looks like. Each painting will be totally unique.

Once you have made your spin art paintings, have fun turning them into bright and colorful birds. No two spin art birds will be the same!

SUPPLIES

Scissors

White poster board

9½-inch (24-cm) wide or larger manual salad spinner

Red, orange, light yellow, dark yellow, green, light blue, dark blue and purple water-based tempera paints

6 large googly eyes

Yellow or orange craft foam

White glue

Feathers, 2 red, 2 blue and 2 yellow

STEP 1: PREPARE YOUR POSTER BOARD

Begin by cutting three 5 x 5–inch (13 x 13–cm) circles from the white poster board. Then put one of the circles at the bottom of your salad spinner.

STEP 2: ADD SOME PAINT

Squirt small blobs of paint on top of the circle of poster board inside the salad spinner. For the red bird, use red and orange paint; for the blue bird, use light blue, dark blue and purple paint; and for the yellow bird, use light yellow, dark yellow and green paint. You can squirt the paints straight from their bottles.

Start with two or three small squirts of each color. Try to space the blobs of paint out, ensuring some paint is near the center of the circle. You can add more paint later if you would like to.

STEP 3: SPIN, SPIN, SPIN!

Place the lid firmly on the salad spinner and get ready to spin. This is where the fun really begins!

Spin the salad spinner as fast as you can for about 20 seconds and then remove the lid. As you remove the lid, you will see that the paint colors have spun across the poster board circle and in some cases mixed together.

If you are happy with your spin art, remove it from the salad spinner and allow it to dry. Alternatively, experiment with adding a few more squirts of paint and spin it again.

STEP 4: TURN YOUR SPIN ART INTO COLORFUL BIRDS

When your spin art has dried, it is time to make your birds. Give each bird two googly eyes and cut out small triangles from orange or yellow craft foam to make bird beaks. Glue the eyes and beaks in place.

Then glue two red feathers on the red bird, two blue feathers on the blue bird and two yellow feathers on the yellow bird.

LARGE TAPE RESIST MOSAIC

Go big with this tape resist mosaic project. Tape resist art is easy to set up and looks so pretty. You can take it outdoors to give yourself more space or do it indoors on a rainy day.

SUPPLIES

Large piece cardboard

Painter's tape

Red, orange, yellow, light green, dark green and blue water-based tempera paints or any colors of your choice

Paint pots (one for each color)

Paintbrushes (one for each color)

STEP 1: PREPARE YOUR CARDBOARD

Dig through your recycling bin to find the largest piece of cardboard you have. Then use painter's tape to section off small areas of the cardboard at various angles. You are aiming to have the whole piece of cardboard sectioned off into various-sized shapes. Use two different widths of painter's tape to add extra interest. Make sure the painter's tape is pressed down firmly so no paint can seep underneath. Now your mosaic is ready for painting.

STEP 2: PAINT EACH SECTION

Use a selection of brightly colored paints to paint each section of the mosaic. Use one color for each section. Don't worry too much if the paint colors end up mixing, as this can create a desirable effect. Use whatever color combination you feel will work best, and try to spread the colors out across the mosaic so that each section is different.

STEP 3: REMOVE THE TAPE

Once you have finished painting each section, get ready to remove the painter's tape to reveal your final mosaic.

Once the tape has been removed, you can marvel at the beautiful mosaic you have created!

ADAPT THE PROJECT

This project works really well on a smaller scale too. You can also get a little more adventurous by taping off the shape of the first letter of your name or of a simple shape like a heart.

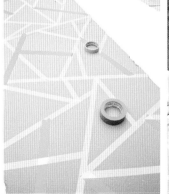

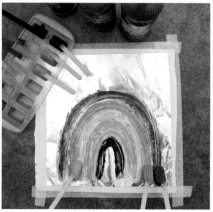

ICE PAINTING ON FOIL

Make a set of colorful ice paints and use them to paint on foil. Foil is a really interesting alternative canvas, and it's a lot of fun gliding ice paints across it. Paint a simple picture with your ice paints and take a print, or have fun mixing colors and exploring what happens to the ice paints as they start to melt. The choice is yours!

SUPPLIES

Red, orange, yellow, green, blue and purple water-based tempera paints

Ice cube tray

Small Jug

Water

Craft sticks

Freezer

Foil

White mixed-media paper (optional)

STEP 1: MAKE YOUR ICE PAINTS

Squirt paint straight from the bottles into an ice cube tray. Use a different paint color in each ice cube mold, filling each about halfway with paint. Then top off each mold with a little water and mix the paint and water together using craft sticks. Leave a craft stick in each mold and then place the tray in the freezer overnight or until frozen.

STEP 2: PAINT TIME!

Once your ice paints have frozen, take them out of the freezer and run the back of the ice cube tray under some warm water to help release the paints.

Set up your workspace with your ice paints and a piece of foil, then have fun gliding your ice paints across the foil. The paints can be a little harder to use when they first come out of the ice cube tray, but they will quickly begin to melt a little and are easy to paint with.

Use your ice paints to paint a picture or make patterns on your foil or have fun exploring what happens as you mix two or three colors together. The texture of the ice paints changes as they begin to melt, which can also be interesting to explore.

STEP 3: MAKE A PRINT (OPTIONAL)

Taking a print of your artwork is easy. Simply lay a piece of paper on top of your ice painting, press firmly and then peel back the paper to reveal your print.

ADAPT THE PROJECT

Ice paints can also be made using food coloring and water. To make this version, add water to your ice cube tray along with a few drops of food coloring and a craft stick in each cube mold. Freeze the tray and remove the ice cube paints once they are frozen solid. While these ice paints can't be used on foil, they look great on paper.

COTTON PAD SNAILS

Turn an ordinary cotton pad into an adorable little snail. This painting project couldn't be any simpler, and it looks so cute. But why make just one snail when you can experiment with different color combinations and make a whole collection of snails?

SUPPLIES

White glue

Cotton pads

1 (25½ x 38-inch [65 x 96-cm]) piece cardboard

Black marker

Liquid watercolor paints in any colors of your choice

Paint palette

Pipette or thick paintbrush

STEP 1: DRAW YOUR SNAIL

Start by gluing a cotton pad in the center of your cardboard piece. Then turn it into a snail by drawing the bottom part of the snail using a black marker. The cotton pad will become the snail's shell.

STEP 2: PAINT THE SNAIL'S SHELL

Prepare your watercolor paints on a palette. You may want to water down your liquid watercolor paints so the colors are less concentrated and they go further. Use a pipette to carefully squirt your watercolor paint onto the cotton pad. The cotton pad will absorb the paint and quickly be filled with color. If you don't have a pipette, you can use a thick paintbrush instead.

ADAPT THE PROJECT

You don't have to just stick to snails. Try making other pictures too. You could add wings and a beak to make a bird, a head and legs to make a turtle or petals to make a flower.

TOP TIP

Use two or three colors of paint and see what happens as they mix together.

OUTDOOR INTERACTIVE PAINTING

Get outdoors and get messy with these fun, interactive painting ideas. Not only will you have fun splatting and spreading paint, but you will make some beautiful wall-worthy artwork in the process.

From squirting paint-filled water pistols (page 84) and creating colorful canvases, to experimenting with paint pouring on a set of terra-cotta pots (page 92) and making your own fizzy paints (page 104), you are going to have trouble deciding which of these fun ideas to try first.

Just a word of warning: Most of these ideas are really messy, so make sure you wear old clothes and either find an area outdoors you are happy to make extra colorful or cover your workspace with a large piece of plastic or cloth.

WATER GUN PAINTING

Create some wall-worthy artwork by squirting color onto a large canvas with a paint-filled water gun! This abstract painting technique is so much fun, and the unique piece of artwork you create will grab everyone's attention.

SUPPLIES

3 small water guns

Yellow, green and blue or red, blue and purple water-based tempera paints

Water

Small jugs

1 (18 x 23½-inch [46 x 60-cm]) large canvas

Easel (optional)

ADAPT THE PROJECT

If you don't have a canvas for this project, it can also be made on paper. Attach the paper to an easel or wall and get squirting!

STEP 1: PREPARE YOUR WATER GUNS

Before heading outdoors to start painting, you will need to prepare your water guns. You will need one water gun for each paint color you plan to use.

I suggest using three different paint colors. Red, blue and purple work well, as do yellow, green and blue, but feel free to have fun experimenting with other color combinations.

To prepare your watery paint, start by mixing equal parts of your chosen paint color and water together in a jug. The amount of watery paint you will need will vary slightly depending on the size of your water guns, but I suggest starting off by mixing ½ cup (120 ml) of paint and ½ cup (120 ml) of water.

Pour your watery paint mixture from the jug into your water gun. Then secure the cap on the water gun and give the water gun a shake to make sure the paint and water are completely mixed together. Repeat for each color.

STEP 2: PAINTING TIME!

Once your water guns are filled with watery paint, it is time to set up your canvas and get ready to paint.

Prop your canvas up in an open outdoor area on an easel or against a tree or wall. Make sure it is in an area that you are happy to get messy or cover your surface with plastic so it can easily be cleaned of any paint that misses the canvas.

Step back from the canvas, aim your water gun and get ready to fire!

Have fun squirting the different colored paints at the canvas. Watch as the canvas begins to fill with splats of paint and they start to run down the canvas. Experiment with squirting your water gun at close range and from a distance as well as from different angles. Observe as the paint colors start to mix together to create new colors.

Once you have finished your painting, lay it flat to dry and then hang it up with pride.

PAINTING ON A SLIDE

Rolling objects covered in paint down a slide is such a simple painting project but great fun. Yes, it gets messy, but isn't that the best part? If you don't have any toy cars, don't panic. You can experiment with other round objects that will roll instead.

SUPPLIES

Large roll of paper

Slide or ramp

Tape

Red, blue and yellow water-based tempera paints

Small tray

3 or more small toy cars, small balls or natural objects

TOP TIP

If you don't have a slide, set up a ramp. You can do this by placing a piece of cardboard or wood at an angle against a hard vertical surface like a wall or fence.

STEP 1: PREPARE YOUR SLIDE

Use a large roll of paper to cover the length of your slide, ensuring you tape it into place. The cars will run off the end of the slide, so make sure you set up your slide in an area you are happy to get messy or protect your surface with a piece of plastic that can be wiped clean.

Then squirt red, blue and yellow paint into your tray. You will need a thin layer of each color, enough to cover the wheels on your toy cars. Place the tray of paint at the top of your slide.

STEP 2: TIME TO PAINT!

One by one, dip your toy cars into the tray of paint so the wheels are covered in paint, and then place them at the top of the slide. As you push the cars with paint on their wheels down the slide, take a look at the colorful track marks made.

Repeat using all three colors and then collect the cars. Re-dip them in the paint and get ready to go again.

STEP 3: USE YOUR PAINTING (OPTIONAL)

This painting project is more about enjoying the painting process than about what the final painting looks like, but that doesn't mean you won't end up with some interesting artwork.

The large roll of paper you use for this project could be repurposed into homemade wrapping paper.

ADAPT THE PROJECT

While toy cars work well for this project, so do many other objects. Try out a few different round objects like small balls or pinecones to see which you like painting with best. You may also like to experiment with different color combinations.

BUBBLE PAINTING POTIONS

Go crazy making colorful bubbly potions! You are going to love this exciting way of painting using bottles of colored bubble solution. What types of potions will you make?

Bubble painting might look like it isn't too messy, but it definitely is, because the bubbles end up all over the place. Wear old clothes and protect your workspace before you begin.

SUPPLIES

1 sheet white mixed-media paper

Permanent marker

6 bottles bubble solution with wands

Small jug

Red, blue, purple, green, yellow and orange liquid watercolor paints or food coloring

STEP 1: DRAW YOUR POTION BOTTLES

Draw a large potion bottle on the paper with a permanent marker. If you want to make more than one potion, draw each bottle on a separate piece of paper.

You can make your potion bottle any shape you like. Make it round, straight or shaped like a flask or test tube, the choice is yours. You may also like to draw a simple picture or add a label on your bottle to give a clue as to what potion is inside.

STEP 2: PREPARE YOUR BUBBLES

To prepare your colored bubble mixture, pour about a quarter of the bubble solution out of each bottle. You can keep the spare mixture in a small jug for later use.

Then add 10 to 15 drops of liquid watercolor paint to each bottle of bubbles and stir the mixture with the bubble wand. Use one bottle of bubbles for each color. If you feel your colors aren't as bright as you would like, add more drops of liquid watercolor.

STEP 3: READY, SET, BLOW!

Now you are ready to fill your potion bottles with bubbly magic potions! Dip the bubble wand into one of the prepared solutions. Then blow the bubbles over your potion bottle. As the paint splatters and the bubbles pop, you will be left with a wonderful bubbly pattern on your paper.

Continue using several colors until you feel your bubbly potion is complete. Repeat this process for any additional potion bottles you have drawn.

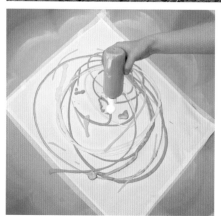

PAINTING IN A KIDDIE POOL

Mix things up a little and instead of cooling down in your kiddie pool use it for painting!
This is a great painting project to do with a few friends.

SUPPLIES

Scissors

Large roll of paper

Small kiddie pool or a large cardboard box

Tape

Water-based tempera paints in pastel colors or any colors of your choice

5 or more small balls

STEP 1: PREPARE YOUR KIDDIE POOL

Cut the large roll of paper to the size of the base of your kiddie pool and tape the paper along the base.

A small plastic kiddie pool works really well for this painting project, but a blow-up pool will also work, or you could even use a large cardboard box.

Squirt pastel-color paints onto the paper at the bottom of the kiddie pool. Be generous with the paint and squirt each color in all directions.

STEP 2: PAINTING TIME!

Now it is time to add several balls to the kiddie pool. The idea is to move the balls around the kiddie pool by lifting it up and tipping it. You will need at least two people to help tip it.

As the balls move around the kiddie pool, they will drag paint with them, creating some interesting lines and patterns on your paper. Watch the colors mix, and have fun with your friends!

ADAPT THE PROJECT

This project can also be done on a much smaller scale. Instead of using a kiddie pool, try doing it in a small cardboard box with marbles.

Once you have made your painting, have a go at making some bunting with it. To do this, cut the dried painting into small triangle shapes and tape the pieces to a length of string. Hang your bunting in the garden to add a little color on a sunny afternoon.

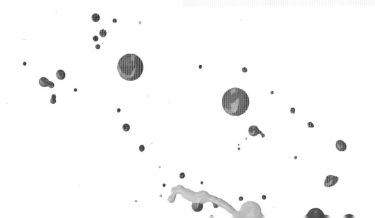

POUR PAINTING
TERRA-COTTA POTS

Brighten up your home with these colorful little plant pots. If you have never tried pour painting before, now is the time! It is such a fun and easy painting technique, and the results look awesome.

SUPPLIES

3 small terra-cotta pots

White acrylic paint and any other colors of your choice

Paintbrush

Cardboard or newspaper, to protect your workspace

Cooling rack

Water (optional)

3 small houseplants

Garden trowel

Potting soil

STEP 1: PAINT YOUR TERRA-COTTA POTS

Start by painting the terra-cotta pots white. You may need two coats of paint to completely cover them. Let them dry.

STEP 2: POUR PAINT ONTO THE TERRA-COTTA POTS

Now for the fun part! You are going to carefully pour paint over the white pots. To avoid making too much mess, place cardboard or newspaper under a cooling rack. Turn the pots upside down on top of the cooling rack.

Now carefully pour paint in colors of your choice straight from the bottles onto the pots so that the paints dribble down the sides. The paint will run off the pots and through the cooling rack onto the newspaper or cardboard below.

If you find your paints are too thick and they are not dribbling down your pots easily, mix the paints with a little water to get a better consistency.

Keep pouring more paint onto the pots until you have paint on all sides. Then allow them to dry. This may take several hours, or even days, depending on the amount of paint used.

STEP 3: ADD PLANTS

Once the paint has dried, remove the pots from the cooling rack and pot a plant of your choice in each one. Then all that's left to do is find the perfect spot to keep your new trio of plants.

EGG SPLAT ART

Not only is egg splat art a lot of fun, but the paintings you make will look amazing when hung up on the wall. Depending on your color choices, you can make them to match any room.

SUPPLIES

10 or more eggshells

Empty egg carton

Water-based tempera paints in various bright colors

Plastic tablecloth, to protect your workspace

1 large canvas in a size of your choice

STEP 1: PREPARE YOUR EGGSHELLS

You will need at least 10 eggshells for this painting project. So as not to waste any eggs, I suggest collecting the eggshells over several days after you have used eggs for cooking. Be careful when you break the eggs, as you only want to crack a small amount off the top of each eggshell (leaving you with about three-quarters of each eggshell).

Wash out the eggshells and allow them to dry. Then place them in an empty egg carton. Half fill each eggshell with paint by squirting it straight from the bottle. Use a variety of different brightly colored paints.

STEP 2: PREPARE THE PAINTING AREA

This is a very messy project, so cover the area you are planning to paint in with a large plastic tablecloth. You will need to choose an area that has a wall, fence or hedge that you can prop your canvas against, or alternatively, you can use an easel.

Once you have propped up your canvas, step back and throw the eggshells filled with paint at the canvas. As they hit the canvas, they will break and splatter the canvas with paint. Repeat with all of the paint-filled eggshells.

When you have finished throwing all the eggs, check if any eggshells still have paint in them. If they do, you can throw them at your canvas a second time.

Pick off any pieces of eggshell left on your painting and then allow it to dry flat.

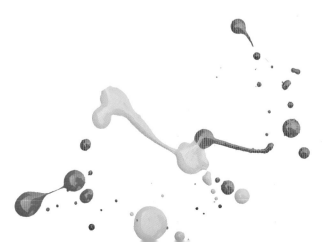

LEAF SILHOUETTE SPRAY PAINTING

Make your own spray paint by filling a spray bottle with watered-down paint.
You can use your spray paint to paint all kinds of things, but it is especially great
to use for creating silhouettes.

SUPPLIES

Leaves

2 small spray bottles
(one for each color)

Light green and dark
green water-based
tempera paints

Water

Scissors

1 sheet white mixed-
media paper

ADAPT THE PROJECT

You can use this technique to create silhouettes of all sorts of objects, from flowers and keys to kitchen utensils. You can even create a silhouette of your hand if you can keep it still while someone sprays around it!

STEP 1: COLLECT LEAVES

Head outdoors and go on a nature walk to find a variety of interesting leaves. Look for different sizes and shapes, and try to choose leaves that you think will lie flat.

STEP 2: MIX UP YOUR SPRAY PAINT

Half fill each spray bottle with paint, one with light green paint and one with dark green paint. Then top the bottles up with water, put the lids on and give them a good shake.

STEP 3: TIME TO PAINT!

Cut the paper into a variety of different sizes and then lay the leaves on top. You might have one leaf on a piece of paper or several laid out to create a pattern.

Make sure the leaves are lying flat on the paper and then spray your light and dark green spray paints over them from above.

Once you have sprayed around the edge of the leaves carefully remove them to reveal their white silhouettes.

PENDULUM PAINTING

This has to be one of my favorite outdoor painting ideas, as it definitely has a wow factor and is mesmerizing to watch. Have fun experimenting with changing the direction and speed of the pendulum to make different patterns.

SUPPLIES

3 bamboo poles

String

Plastic squeeze bottle with a nozzle

Sharp scissors or a craft knife (adults only)

Water

Water-based tempera paints in any 2 colors of your choice

2 jugs

1 large sheet of poster board or canvas

STEP 1: MAKE YOUR PENDULUM

Start by making a tripod to hold the paint container. Tie 3 bamboo poles together about 4 inches (10 cm) from the top. Spread out the poles into a tripod shape and twist string around the area you have tied to make sure the bamboo poles stay in place. If you are setting up your tripod on grass or dirt, you can also push the bamboo poles into the ground to help secure them.

To make the paint container, cut the bottom off the plastic squeeze bottle. You will only need the top portion of the bottle with the nozzle attached for this project. Ask an adult to make a small hole on either side of the cut end with sharp scissors or a craft knife.

Tie a long piece of string to the holes and hang it underneath your tripod. This will be the paint container pendulum. It needs to rest about 2 inches (5 cm) from the ground. You can adjust the string length if needed.

STEP 2: MIX UP YOUR PAINT

Mix together one part water with two parts paint to create a paint that will flow easily through the nozzle of the pendulum. You may need to adjust the exact amount of water to add to your paint, as paint consistency can vary between brands.

Mix the paint and water together in a jug so that the paint can easily be poured into your pendulum when you are ready. You can use any colors of your choice, but I suggest using at least two colors.

STEP 3: TIME TO PAINT

Lay down a large sheet of poster board or a canvas under your tripod. Pour one color of paint into the pendulum container. Pull the container to one side, open the nozzle and let it go.

Watch as the pendulum swings back and forth to create patterns. When you are ready, nudge the container slightly to create a different pattern, or experiment with swinging it faster.

When your first paint color has run out, pour in your second color and watch as new patterns are made on top of the earlier ones.

PAINTING ON ICE

Whether you are doing it to cool down in the summer or using freshly frozen ice in the winter, there is something rather satisfying about painting on ice. While this project doesn't result in artwork you can keep, painting on ice is a wonderful process that's both relaxing and fun.

SUPPLIES

Small tray

Water

Freezer

Watercolor paints

Jar of water, for rinsing brushes

Paintbrushes

STEP 1: PREPARE YOUR ICE

There are two ways that you can prepare the ice for this project. In the winter, if you have very low temperatures outdoors at night, you can fill a tray with water and leave it outside overnight to freeze. Alternatively, you can fill a small tray with water and place it in the freezer overnight. If you have shaped baking trays, use them to add extra interest.

Once your ice is ready, place the tray containing the ice on a table, along with some watercolor paints, a jar of water and some paintbrushes.

STEP 2: PAINT ON THE ICE

Now it is time to have fun painting on the ice! Simply paint watercolors on top of the ice to create patterns and watch what happens as the ice starts melting. Watch as the colors and the texture of the ice change.

ADAPT THE PROJECT

Another slightly different, but equally fun, surface to paint on is snow. Next time you have snow, fill a small tray with it and have fun exploring what it is like to paint it!

PAINTING ON PLASTIC WRAP

Create large-scale outdoor art by painting on plastic wrap. Plastic wrap is easy to remove, which makes it a great temporary canvas. It is easy to set up a canvas of plastic wrap anywhere, so be inventive. Maybe paint in the woods or at the beach. Because the plastic wrap is transparent, the scenery around you becomes part of your artwork.

This painting project is fun to do on your own, but think about how much fun it would be to do with a group of family or friends!

SUPPLIES

2 wooden posts or natural posts, like trees

Plastic wrap

Water-based tempera paints in any colors of your choice

Paint pots (one for each color)

Paintbrushes

STEP 1: SET UP YOUR PLASTIC WRAP

First, find the perfect location for your painting. You will need to either take with you or find two posts that you can wrap the plastic wrap around. Doing this project in the woods works really well, as you can use trees as your posts.

Once you have your two posts, wrap the plastic wrap around them tightly several times. You need it to be strong enough to paint on, but still transparent.

Pick a still day to set up this activity if you can. Trying to set up the plastic wrap on a windy day will be more difficult.

STEP 2: GET PAINTING!

Once the plastic wrap is set up, you are ready to start painting. Have several pots of paint in various colors laid out on the ground below the plastic wrap and get ready to be creative. You can paint what you can see, patterns, shapes or pictures—the choice is yours!

When you have finished your painting, take a photograph to capture it and then take down and remove the plastic wrap.

ADAPT THE PROJECT

If you love this painting project and think you will do it again and again, you might want to invest in a transparent plastic tablecloth that you can use to paint on, wash and reuse.

FIZZY FIREWORKS

I'm not sure which part of this painting project is more fun: mixing up your own homemade paints, painting pictures and patterns on the ground or making the paint fizz up. I think maybe the answer is all of it!

Fizzy fireworks are great fun to paint and watch as they fizz up, but don't feel you need to stick to drawing fireworks. Mix it up a little and try out some other patterns or shapes too.

SUPPLIES

Large jug

2 cups (360 g) baking soda

1 cup (120 g) cornstarch

1 cup (240 ml) water, plus more as needed

Small bowls or a muffin tin

Food coloring in any colors of your choice

Hard surface, such as a driveway or sidewalk

Thick paintbrush

White vinegar

Plastic squeeze bottle

STEP 1: MAKE YOUR OUTDOOR PAINT

In a large jug, combine the baking soda, cornstarch and water and give it a good stir. If the mixture seems hard to mix, add more water a little at a time.

Pour the mixture into several bowls or a muffin tin. In each bowl or muffin cup, add two or three drops of food coloring and mix it in. Your outdoor paint is now ready to use.

STEP 2: PAINT FIREWORKS

Choose a hard surface on the ground to paint your fireworks designs. Use a thick paintbrush to scoop up your homemade paint and paint firework shapes or drip the paint to make it look like sparks.

STEP 3: MAKE YOUR FIREWORKS FIZZ

When you have painted a few fireworks, have fun making them fizz! Pour vinegar into a plastic squeeze bottle and use it to squirt the fireworks you have painted. As the vinegar touches the paint, it will fizz up and cause your fireworks painting to really come to life.

CREATE A MASTERPIECE

Be inspired by the great artists of the world and learn to paint like the masters! In this chapter, you'll explore the artwork of ten famous artists. Using their paintings as inspiration, or using the same techniques as these famous artists, have fun creating your own masterpieces in a similar style.

Maybe you will be inspired by the work of Georges Seurat and enter the world of pointillism (page 116), or perhaps you would prefer to relax as you paint circles inspired by Wassily Kandinsky (page 115). If you have real flowers on hand, maybe the sunflower painting inspired by Vincent van Gogh (page 108) that uses real flowers is for you.

Once you have created your own version of a few of these masterpieces, how about setting up a mini art gallery to showcase your artwork? You could set it up in your house or outdoors and invite family and friends to come and view.

SUNFLOWERS

INSPIRED BY VINCENT VAN GOGH

Van Gogh's still life paintings of sunflowers are among his most famous. The sunflowers were meant to symbolize gratitude.

Create your own sunflower painting with a little twist using paint, cardboard and some real flowers. While this artwork won't last forever—except in a photograph—it looks so pretty!

SUPPLIES

Pencil

Thick piece cardboard

Yellow, light blue, white and brown acrylic paints

Paintbrushes

Paint palette

Scissors

Yellow chrysanthemums or other small, real yellow flowers

ADAPT THE PROJECT

Instead of using real flowers, you could paint small sunflowers on a piece of paper, cut them out and then glue them onto your vase.

STEP 1: PAINT A VASE AND BACKGROUND

With a pencil, draw a vase toward the bottom center of your piece of cardboard. Then draw a horizontal line near the bottom of your cardboard piece to separate the background and the surface the vase is sitting on.

Paint the bottom section with yellow acrylic paint. Use a generous amount of paint and small brushstrokes.

Then paint the top half of the vase yellow. Paint the bottom of the vase a lighter yellow by mixing white into some yellow paint. Add highlights to the vase with an even lighter shade of yellow paint that is almost white. To complete the vase, outline it with brown paint.

Paint the background light blue. Again, be generous with the amount of paint you use so you can see the brushstrokes. Lastly, paint a brown line separating the blue and yellow paint. Allow the paint to dry.

STEP 2: MAKE HOLES IN THE CARDBOARD

Now it is time to think about where you want the flowers to be on your painting. Push the end of a paintbrush through the cardboard to create holes in each space you would like a flower.

STEP 3: ADD REAL FLOWERS

Cut the stems on your flowers so that they are just slightly longer than the thickness of your cardboard. Then push the flowers through the holes you made in step 2. You have now made your real flower vase of yellow flowers.

WATER LILIES

INSPIRED BY CLAUDE MONET

Many of Claude Monet's paintings are of water lilies. He often painted the same scene from different angles and in different lights. He painted more than 250 paintings for his series of water lilies.

Have a go at making your own 3D water lilies masterpiece using a couple of fun painting techniques.

SUPPLIES

Paintbrushes

Water, for making wash and rinsing brushes

2 sheets white mixed-media paper

Blue and green liquid watercolor paints

Knife (adults only)

Lemon

Pink and green water-based tempera paints

Apple

Pencil

Scissors

White glue

STEP 1: PAINT YOUR POND

Brush over your paper with water so it is slightly damp. Then fill the page with blue liquid watercolor paint. Create a little bit of variety by adding areas of green with the green watercolor paint.

Ask an adult to cut a lemon in half, and while the watercolor paint is still wet, drip lemon juice onto the paint. This will create a really unique effect. Allow it to dry.

While you wait, paint a piece of paper with pink tempera paint. You will need this for step 3.

STEP 2: ADD LILY PADS

Half an apple makes the perfect lily pad shape. Ask an adult to cut an apple in half vertically, then dip it into green tempera paint. Use the apple as a stamp to print three lily pads onto your pond.

STEP 3: MAKE YOUR FLOWERS

On the back of the pink paper you painted in step 1, draw a large 2¼-inch (6-cm) flower and a smaller 1½-inch (4-cm) flower. Each flower should have 5 pointy petals. Cut the flowers out and use them as templates to make two more flowers in each size. Fold the petals upward and glue a smaller flower inside each larger flower.

STEP 4: PUT YOUR WATER LILIES PAINTING TOGETHER

Now all that is left to do is to glue the paper flowers onto the lily pads on your pond. Your 3D water lilies painting is now complete!

COLORFUL RECTANGLES

INSPIRED BY PIET MONDRIAN

Piet Mondrian is well known for his use of black horizontal and vertical lines in his paintings that create rectangles in various shapes and sizes. He then used just the primary colors—red, blue and yellow—along with black and white to fill in the rectangles. Get your paints ready and follow in Piet Mondrian's footsteps to create a masterpiece in his signature style.

SUPPLIES

Black, red, blue and yellow water-based tempera paints

Paint palette

Paintbrushes

Jar of water, for washing brushes

Ruler or thick poster board with a straight edge

1 sheet white mixed-media paper

STEP 1: PAINT BLACK HORIZONTAL AND VERTICAL LINES

Squirt black paint onto a large paint palette and use a paintbrush to spread it out so you have a thin, even layer of paint.

Dip your ruler (or the straight edge of a piece of poster board) into the black paint, making sure it is coated evenly.

Then press the ruler covered in paint onto your piece of paper to print a vertical or horizontal line. Repeat this process to fill your paper with lots of vertical or horizontal lines. As you add more lines, you will start to create several rectangles in various sizes.

STEP 2: PAINT THE RECTANGLES

Once your black lines have dried, paint the rectangles using red, blue, yellow and black paint.

Each rectangle needs to be painted with just one of the colors, and you will want to leave some rectangles white.

There is no right or wrong way to do this, some of Mondrian's paintings had lots of colorful rectangles and some were mainly white with just a few rectangles painted.

ADAPT THE PROJECT

Another fun way to create black horizonal and vertical lines is to use black tape. If you go for this option, you won't need to wait for paint to dry before painting the rectangles.

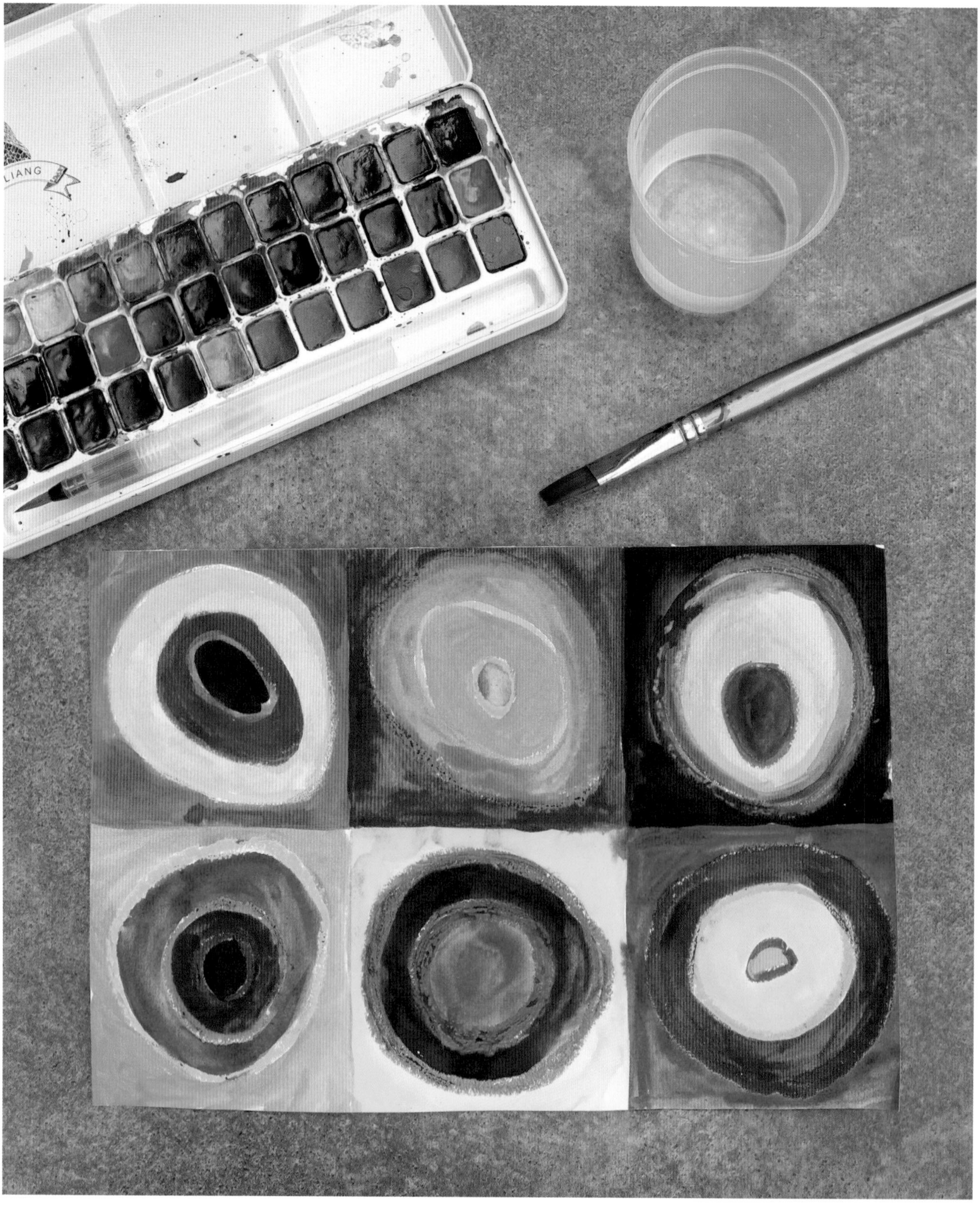
LIANG

CIRCLE ART
INSPIRED BY WASSILY KANDINSKY

Have fun exploring colors and shapes with this relaxing circle art project. Inspired by Kandinsky's Squares with Concentric Circles, this watercolor painting encourages you to explore color mixing and different color combinations. Thanks to Kandinsky's abstract style, there is no right or wrong way to approach this art project, so put on some music, relax and enjoy an afternoon of painting!

SUPPLIES

Ruler

Pencil

1 (7½ x 11–inch [19 x 28–cm]) piece white mixed-media paper

Oil pastels in bright, bold colors

Watercolor paints in bright, bold colors

Paintbrushes

Jar of water, for washing brushes

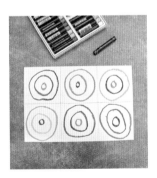

STEP 1: PREPARE YOUR PAPER

Prepare your paper by using a ruler and pencil to divide it into 3¾-inch (9-cm) squares. You can adjust the size of the squares if you want to use a larger or smaller paper.

STEP 2: DRAW YOUR CIRCLES

In each square, use an oil pastel to draw a circle that is large enough to almost go to the edge of the square. Inside that circle, draw another circle that is slightly smaller and another circle that is slightly smaller still. Draw each circle using a different brightly colored oil pastel.

STEP 3: PAINT YOUR CIRCLES

Now it is time to start painting your circles. When choosing your watercolors, try to choose bold and bright colors as Kandinsky did. Have fun mixing up new colors and experimenting with how different colors work alongside one another.

Paint each of the circles in bright colors, making sure the same colors do not touch. Once you are happy with your painted circles, complete the squares around them with different colors. When you have finished, there should be no white left on your piece of paper.

ADAPT THE PROJECT

This circle color study can be navigated in so many ways! Experiment with different colors and different types of paint.

If painting six squares full of circles is too much, how about turning it into a group project by persuading a few family and friends to join in painting some circles? Glue each square full of circles down next to one another on a piece of poster board to display.

POINTILLISM
INSPIRED BY GEORGES SEURAT

Have you ever tried dot painting? It is surprisingly easy! Georges Seurat is well known for using pointillism in his paintings. Instead of blending colors on his palette, he used lots of tiny strokes of color that blend together when you look at them from a distance. Are you ready to have a go at creating a picture using this pointillism technique?

SUPPLIES

Pencil

1 (5 x 6-inch [13 x 15-cm]) piece white mixed-media paper

Gray, white, brown, gold, dark blue and light blue acrylic paints

Paint palette

Cotton swabs

6 x 7-inch (15 x 18-cm) piece cardboard (optional)

White glue (optional)

String (optional)

STEP 1: DRAW YOUR PICTURE

Using a pencil, draw a boat, or any other picture or scene you would like to try, onto your paper.

STEP 2: ADD DOTS OF PAINT

Now you are going to fill the picture with dots of paint. An easy way to do this is with cotton swabs. Simply dip the swabs into the paint and then onto your paper to create perfect little dots.

For the sail, start with gray dots of paint and then add white dots. For the base of the boat, start with brown and then add gold dots. For the background, start with dark blue dots and then add light blue dots.

STEP 3: FRAME YOUR PAINTING (OPTIONAL)

Make your pointillism painting stand out by gluing it onto a cardboard frame. To hang your frame, poke two small holes at the top of your cardboard and thread string through them. Tie the string and get ready to hang your painting.

ADAPT THE PROJECT

If you want to keep things simple, you can use one color of dots for each section instead of two.

POP ART

INSPIRED BY ANDY WARHOL

Andy Warhol liked making prints, as it meant he could easily produce the same image lots of times. He often used repeated images of everyday items like cans of soup and of celebrities like Marilyn Monroe. Sometimes he would play with color and use different colors each time he made a print. Have a go at making your own print using polystyrene, and print it lots of times on different-colored backgrounds.

SUPPLIES

Pencil

1 (4 x 5½–inch [10 x 14–cm]) piece polystyrene

Black acrylic paint or printing ink

Paint tray

Paint roller

4 sheets colored paper: 1 pink, 1 green, 1 blue and 1 yellow

White poster board

STEP 1: MAKE YOUR STAMP

Decide on the subject matter you would like to use for your print. A few suggestions are a self-portrait, a favorite animal, flowers or leaves, hearts or simple food items like cupcakes. Whatever subject matter you choose, you need to keep your design simple.

Use a pencil to carve your design into the polystyrene. You will need to press down with a fair amount of pressure to create deep lines. As you are creating your stamp, bear in mind that the lines you have drawn are the parts of your stamp that will not have any paint applied to them. Also be aware that the image on your stamp will be reversed.

STEP 2: MAKE YOUR PRINTS

Add a few squirts of black acrylic paint or printing ink to a paint tray and roll the paint out using a roller. Then roll the black paint over your polystyrene stamp, ensuring you have an even layer of paint.

Place the stamp over your colored paper and press it down with firm, even pressure. Carefully peel off the polystyrene to reveal your print.

Repeat this process on each of the colored papers.

STEP 3: PUT THE PRINTS TOGETHER

Once your prints have dried, glue them next to one another on a piece of poster board or on a canvas. Your colorful pop art is now complete!

PAINTED PAPER COLLAGE

INSPIRED BY HENRI MATISSE

Grab some scissors and some painted paper and take pleasure in cutting out organic shapes just like Matisse. Henri Matisse is well known for his abstract collages made from painted paper. Be inspired by his work and cover your own paper with beautiful colored shapes.

SUPPLIES

7 sheets white mixed-media paper

Red, orange, yellow, light green, dark green and blue water-based tempera paints

Paintbrushes

Scissors

White glue

STEP 1: PAINT YOUR PAPER

Paint each of the 6 sheets of paper a different solid color, using each of the colors noted in the supply list. Don't worry about visible brushstrokes; these will add to the overall painted paper effect. Allow your paper to dry.

STEP 2: CUT OUT ORGANIC SHAPES

On the back of the dry painted papers, draw a variety of organic shapes. Be inspired by Matisse's rounded leaf shapes or come up with your own curved and natural shapes. Then cut out the shapes.

STEP 3: ARRANGE AND GLUE THE SHAPES

Arrange the cutouts on a sheet of white paper, moving them around until you are happy with the composition. When everything is in the right place, glue it down.

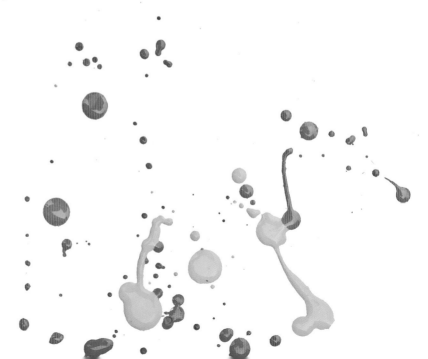

FLOWER PAINTING
INSPIRED BY GEORGIA O'KEEFFE

Georgia O'Keeffe is well known and loved for her flower paintings. She painted close-ups of flowers that extended off the page, and she simplified their shapes, often making them slightly abstract. Look closely at some flowers and try your hand at painting an enlarged flower of your own.

SUPPLIES

Vase of real flowers or images of flowers

1 (6 x 8-inch [15 x 20-cm]) canvas or any size of your choice

Pencil

Acrylic paint in colors to match your inspiration flowers

Paintbrushes

Paint palette

Jar of water, for washing brushes

Magnifying glass (optional)

Paint pens (optional)

STEP 1: DRAW YOUR FLOWER

Set up a vase of flowers and place your canvas on the table or on a small easel next to them.

Look closely at the flowers, using a magnifying glass if your wish, and then draw an enlarged version of part of one flower on your canvas.

Start by drawing the center of the flower and then add the petals, making them large enough that they will go off the edge of the canvas.

STEP 2: PAINT THE FLOWER

Using colors that are similar to the flower you are looking at, paint your flower drawing. Add in any details you see.

When you have finished painting the flower, paint the background in a contrasting color to make the flower really stand out. Use paint pens to add outlines or small details to your painting if you wish.

ADAPT THE PROJECT

Go big! Instead of using a small canvas, grab a huge canvas or sheet of paper and paint a giant close-up flower.

SPLATTER PAINTING
INSPIRED BY JACKSON POLLOCK

Pouring and splashing paint is so much fun, and it is exactly what Jackson Pollock is well known for. He used paints that poured smoothly so they were easy to drip and laid his canvas on the floor so he could move around easily to see all four sides. Use your whole body to paint a masterpiece just like Jackson Pollock. This is action art at its best!

This is going to get very messy so make sure you take this outdoors and find an area you are happy to get covered in paint or cover your workspace well.

SUPPLIES

Paint pots (one for each color)

Water-based tempera paints in any colors of your choice

Water, for diluting paints, if needed

Paintbrushes

1 large canvas in a size of your choice

Small spoons

Sticks

STEP 1: PREPARE YOUR PAINTS

Prepare your paints by pouring them into paint pots that are easy to access.

Pollock used a lot of black and white in his painting with glimpses of other colors such as gray, yellow, blue and pink. Use similar colors to Pollock's or go bright and colorful—the choice is yours.

You need your paints to pour smoothly. Test out the paints you have to make sure they easily run off a spoon, if they don't, add a little water to them to make them runnier.

STEP 2: PAINT YOUR CANVAS (OPTIONAL)

If you would like a colored background for your splatter painting, paint the canvas entirely in one color of your choice.

STEP 3: GET SPLATTING!

Now it is time to place your canvas on the floor, just as Pollock would have done, and have fun splatting, flicking and pouring paint onto your canvas.

Use paintbrushes, small spoons or even sticks to splash the paint onto your canvas. Use your whole body as you move to drip and flick paint from all angles.

Keep splatting and layering the paint until you feel your canvas is complete. Then leave it on a flat surface to dry. Due to the amount of paint used, this might take several days, but once it is dry, it will look amazing hanging on your wall.

FLOWERS IN YOUR HAIR
INSPIRED BY FRIDA KAHLO

Have fun painting with real flowers to create a flower headdress for Frida Kahlo. Frida Kahlo was well known for her many self-portraits in which she often wore flowers in her hair. Either draw a portrait of Frida Kahlo or a self-portrait and decorate it with colorful flower prints.

SUPPLIES

Black marker

1 sheet white mixed-media paper

Mirror (optional)

Red, yellow and green water-based tempera paints or any colors of your choice

Paint palette

Paintbrush

Real flowers in several sizes, if possible

STEP 1: DRAW A PORTRAIT

Using a black marker, draw a portrait of Frida Kahlo or a self-portrait. If doing a self-portrait, you might want to find a small mirror to look at your features as you draw. Leave room at the top of your paper for the flowers. If you are drawing a picture of Frida, don't forget to take a look at a few images of her with flowers in her hair to help you.

STEP 2: ADD FLOWER PRINTS

Squirt a little red, yellow and green paint—and any other colors you would like to use—onto a palette and spread the paint out with a paintbrush. Dip your flowers into the paint, making sure they are covered evenly. Then press the flowers covered with paint onto your paper in the space above your portrait to make a print. Keep adding flower prints until you have painted a full headdress of flowers.

ADAPT THE PROJECT

Instead of drawing a portrait, you could try adding flowers to a photograph of your own face.

IMAGINATIVE MIXED-MEDIA PROJECTS

Mix together different materials or painting techniques to create some unique mixed-media artwork. This chapter is about using your imagination and relaxing as you paint.

From painting the view from your window, or a view you would like to see (page 137), working collaboratively with a group of family or friends to paint a canvas (page 141), to even taking flight with a pair of your very own painted wings (page 134), there are lots of fun ideas to keep you busy.

DESIGN YOUR OWN CASTLE

Let your imagination go into overdrive and be as creative as you can as you design your own magical castle. This is a fun and easy painting project that you can really make your own.

SUPPLIES

2 sheets white mixed-media paper

Light gray, black and dark gray acrylic paints or any colors of your choice

Paint palette

Paintbrushes

Black and red paint pens or markers or other colors of your choice

Ruler

Craft knife (adults only)

Scissors

Small rectangular sponge

White glue

STEP 1: PAINT YOUR PAPER

Paint a sheet of paper light gray, or any other color you would like your castle to be, and allow it to dry. Paint a second piece of paper black.

STEP 2: DRAW YOUR CASTLE

Draw your castle design on your gray painted paper using a black paint pen or marker. Use a ruler to help if you want straight lines, or go freehand. Add towers, windows and a door, as well as flags and anything else you would like included on your castle.

Color in any areas you want to be blacked out, like windows, with your black paint pen. Then use the red paint pen to add small areas of color on the flags.

STEP 3: SPONGE PRINT THE BRICKWORK

Cut a sponge (no need for adult help) into a small rectangle approximately ¾ inch (2 cm) long and an even smaller rectangle approximately ⅓ inch (1 cm) long. Dip them into your dark gray paint and use them to sponge print the brickwork onto your castle design. Use the larger rectangle sponge first and then use the smaller one to fill in any gaps.

STEP 4: MAKE THE DOOR

Allow your painting to dry and then ask an adult to cut around the door with a craft knife so that it can be opened. Glue the black painted paper behind your castle painting so it is dark when the door is opened.

ADAPT THE PROJECT

Try out different designs and colors. Maybe you could make a pink palace or a blue magical castle!

WHAT'S IN THE BACKGROUND?

What's in the background? It can be anything your imagination can think up!

Turn an ordinary photo or image of an animal into something amazing by painting your own background. You could keep it pretty normal and paint a jungle or woodland as your background, or why not make it a little crazier by painting a volcano or magical world behind your animal.

This activity is so much fun and there really is no right or wrong way to tackle it.

SUPPLIES

Image of an animal

White printer paper

Printer

Scissors

White glue

1 sheet white mixed-media paper

Permanent black marker

Watercolor paints in any colors of your choice

Paintbrushes

Jar of water, for washing brushes

STEP 1: FIND AN IMAGE

Search through your photographs or online to find a picture of an animal. This could be a pet, forest animal, jungle animal or any other animal you would like to use. Print out a copy of your chosen image and cut it out. It should be about a quarter of the size of the piece of paper you are going to paint the background on.

STEP 2: PAINT A BACKGROUND

Glue your animal image onto your paper and think about what you might include in the background. Then, using a permanent black marker, draw the outline of your background around the animal. You can include anything you like, so be as imaginative as you can.

Once you are happy with the outline, take out your watercolor paints and paint the background.

If you are going for a jungle background, you could make it look more realistic by painting some leaves and pressing them onto your paper to make leaf prints.

ADAPT THE PROJECT

You don't have to just use animal images. You could use an image of yourself, an object or something that is personal to you to put in the picture.

PAINTED CARDBOARD WINGS

Next time you get a delivery, don't throw the cardboard boxes away.
Cardboard can be perfect for so many painting projects—in this case, making
a set of painted cardboard wings.

What type of wings will you make? Fairy wings, dragon wings or maybe even
an exotic bird's wings? There are so many options to try!

SUPPLIES

Pencil

Large piece cardboard

Scissors

Water-based tempera
paints in bright colors

Paint palette

Clothespins

Items to paint with
(pom-poms, feathers,
sponges, twine, foam,
leaves, etc.)

Ribbon

STEP 1: CUT OUT WING SHAPE

Decide what type of wings you would like to make and draw them onto a
large piece of cardboard.

To make sure both wings are the same shape, fold your cardboard in half and
draw one side of the wings. Cut that wing out and then trace around it on the
other side of the cardboard. Cut out the second wing, making sure that the
wings stay attached to each other.

STEP 2: PAINT YOUR WINGS

Now it is time to paint your wings using lots of bright colors. While you can
use regular paintbrushes to paint your wings, you can make the painting
process even more fun by using your own homemade DIY paintbrushes.

To make DIY paintbrushes, simply clip various items into clothespins. Try
pom-poms, feathers, sponges, twine, foam, leaves or anything else you can
find that you think could make an interesting shape or texture.

STEP 3: WEAR YOUR WINGS

Once the paint has dried, make two small holes on each side of the wings
near the middle. Thread a piece of ribbon that is long enough to fit over your
shoulders through each set of holes and then tie it in place.

You can now wear your wings and go off on an imaginative adventure!

VIEW THROUGH THE WINDOW

What do you see through your window? Use your imagination or paint what you actually see, the choice is yours.

SUPPLIES

1 sheet white mixed-media paper

Painter's tape

Oil pastels in any colors of your choice

Watercolor paints in any colors of your choice

Paintbrushes

Jar of water, for washing brushes

Salt (optional)

STEP 1: TAPE OFF A WINDOW

Make a window frame on your paper using painter's tape. Add strips of tape along each edge of the paper and create a cross shape across the middle.

STEP 2: DRAW THE VIEW THROUGH THE WINDOW

Use oil pastels to draw an outline of the view through your window. This can be real or imaginary. Use bold shapes and lines.

Your drawing will go over the painter's tape, but be mindful of the fact that this part of the picture will be removed later, so don't add anything really important to your picture on the tape.

STEP 3: PAINT YOUR PICTURE

Use your watercolors to paint the different areas of your picture. The oil pastels will resist the paint, keeping the colors separate. While the paper is wet, sprinkle on a little salt to add an interesting texture. Allow your painting to dry.

STEP 4: REMOVE THE PAINTER'S TAPE

Now for the reveal! Once your painting is completely dry, brush off the salt and then remove the painter's tape to see your view through a window frame.

TEXTURED FRAME

Frame your favorite photograph in your own homemade frame. Making a frame from cardboard is really easy, and you can totally customize it by adding various colors, patterns and textures.

SUPPLIES

Picture or photograph

Rectangular piece cardboard, roughly 2 inches (5 cm) larger in length or height than your photo

Pencil

Scissors

Various textured materials (corrugated cardboard, bubble wrap, string, etc.)

White glue

Water-based tempera paints in any colors of your choice

Paint palette

Paintbrushes

STEP 1: MAKE YOUR FRAME

Choose a picture or photograph you would like to frame and find a rectangular piece of cardboard to make the frame out of.

Center your picture on the piece of cardboard and trace the outline onto the cardboard. Then draw a slightly smaller rectangle inside the first and cut this out. You need the hole you are cutting out to be slightly smaller than your photograph or picture so that you are able to glue it in place behind the frame.

Then search through your recycling bin to see what textures you can find to stick on your frame. Things like corrugated cardboard, string and bubble wrap work well.

Glue various textures to the width of your cardboard frame and allow it to dry.

STEP 2: PAINTING TIME!

Once the glue has fully dried, paint your frame. Each texture can be painted a different bright color. Have fun being creative as you decide which colors to use.

Once your frame is dry, glue or tape your picture or photograph behind the cutout.

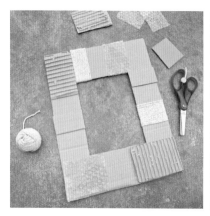

LARGE FAMILY CANVAS

It can be great fun working on a collaborative piece with your family or a group of friends. Listen to some music to inspire you as you all work on your own areas of the canvas. Have fun, relax and see what you come up with.

SUPPLIES

1 large canvas in any size to fit your space

Pencil (optional)

Music

Water-based tempera paints in any colors of your choice

Paint pots

Paintbrushes

Oil pastels, markers or scrapbook paper (optional)

STEP 1: PREPARE YOUR CANVAS AND PAINTS

Put your canvas in the center of a table and arrange the paint and brushes so they can be easily reached on all sides of the table.

When choosing your paint colors, think about where you will be hanging your canvas. Is there already a color scheme in that room that you would like to use? Or do you have a favorite color you would like included?

Drawing simple shapes in pencil on your canvas, like various sized circles, is a great way to get started if you are unsure what to paint.

STEP 2: TIME TO PAINT!

Put on some inspiring music and get ready to paint!

Choose a place on the canvas you would like to start painting, and then when you are ready, trade places around the table to paint in a different area of the canvas. Keep swapping places with your family or friends and keep adding to your painting until you feel it is finished.

STEP 3: HANG YOUR PAINTING WITH PRIDE

When the painting has dried, hang it up to display or add more detail with a second layer of paint or other media, such as oil pastels, markers or scrapbook paper, on top of the paint to add extra texture or detail.

  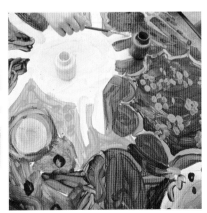

TAKE A LINE FOR A WALK

This is such a calming and relaxing activity. Simply scribble across your page using black glue, and then enjoy painting each area with various colors. Don't overthink it; the colors don't matter. The focus of this activity is to let your mind and body relax and just go with it!

SUPPLIES

Small (4-ounce [118-ml]) bottle white glue with nozzle

Black acrylic paint

Paintbrushes

1 sheet white mixed-media paper

Watercolor paints in various colors

Jar of water, for making washes and rinsing brushes

Paint palette

STEP 1: MAKE YOUR BLACK GLUE

You will be using black glue for this project, but if you don't want to have to wait for the glue to dry, use a black oil pastel or permanent black marker instead.

To make black glue, pour out about 25 percent of the white glue from the bottle, and store it somewhere for future use. Then fill the space left in the bottle with black acrylic paint. Shake it well and then mix it using the end of a paintbrush. Replace the nozzle on the glue bottle, and your black glue is ready to use. You can also use this black glue to make pictures like the Black Glue Resist – *Cactus Painting* on page 63.

STEP 2: DRAW A SCRIBBLE IN BLACK GLUE

Use the black glue to scribble across your paper. Try to use one thin, continuous line of glue. You may need to practice a little first to get used to the flow of the glue. Curve and wiggle the line of glue across the paper. There is no right or wrong way to do this, and each time you try, the result will be different.

Allow the black glue to fully dry.

STEP 3: PAINTING TIME!

Now it is time to grab your watercolor paints and start adding some color to your scribble. Use one paint color for each section. Apply water to each section before adding the paint and watch as the paint spreads out across the water. The black glue will resist the watercolor paint, making it easy to keep the paint within each section. Keep adding paint until the piece of paper is fully colored.

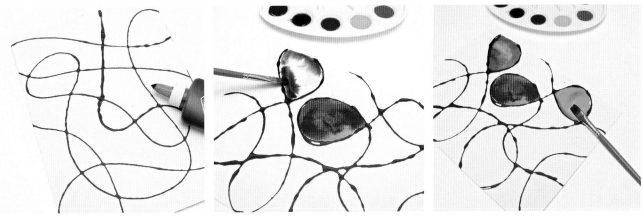

PAINTED PAPER PICTURES

Painted paper pictures can look amazingly eye-catching. Paint some pieces of paper and add fun textures to them using various tools, then use them to make pictures.

Alternatively, you can use some of the painted paper that you have made during previous painting projects in the book—e.g., Bubble Wrap Painting – *Hot Air Balloon* (page 33) and Scrape Painting – *Mini Pictures* (page 68).

SUPPLIES

Water-based tempera paints in various colors

Paintbrushes

Several sheets white mixed-media paper

Tools to make marks in paint (fork, sponge, cardboard, cardboard tube, etc.)

Pencil

Scissors

White glue

STEP 1: PAINT PAPER

Making painted paper is a lot of fun and a great way to experiment with the different marks you can make with paint.

Paint a sheet of paper in a color of your choice, or several colors, and then try making marks in the paint with various tools. Try dragging a fork through the paint to make lines or using the end of a paintbrush to make swirls. Try dabbing the paint with a sponge or flicking splatters of paint.

Repeat using different colors to make several sheets of painted paper. Allow your painted paper to dry.

STEP 2: MAKE A PAINTED PAPER PICTURE

Now use the painted paper to make some pictures. You can make any picture you choose, but I recommend keeping it simple.

Once you have decided on your design, draw the shapes you need on your painted paper. Then cut out the shapes and glue them together on a blank sheet of paper.

ACKNOWLEDGMENTS

Thank you to my family, who inspires and encourages me every day.

To my mum and dad, who have always encouraged me to be creative, have fun with art and crafts and follow my dreams, which has ultimately led to me writing this painting projects book. Special thanks to my mum for taking the time to talk through ideas, read through early drafts and look after the children when I needed some quiet time to write or create.

To my husband, who has supported me, brought me many cups of tea to keep me going and put up with a house full of messy paint pots for the last few months as writing this book has taken over.

To my three children, Harry, Daisy and Ollie, who happily go along with all my crazy art ideas and inspire me with amazing ideas of their own. Without them, there would be no Messy Little Monster website or book. An extra special thank-you for all the wonderful artwork that they have contributed to this book and for being amazing and very patient models. Thank you also to their cousins Jake, Sophie, Elodie and Lars and their friends Rio, Izzabella and Adriana for coming to paint with us.

To all Messy Little Monster readers, for trying out and sharing our crafts and activities. Thank you for your continued support over the years.

To Jen Allan, for the most wonderful photography. I have loved working with you, and you have managed to capture the painting projects perfectly.

To Marissa Giambelluca, Meg Baskis and the whole team at Page Street Publishing, thank you for all your support and for making my dream of writing a book a reality.

ABOUT THE AUTHOR

Louise McMullen is the creator of Messy Little Monster, a popular kids' craft and activity website that is packed with over 1,000 fun activity ideas. Since the website was set up in 2014, millions of children, parents, grandparents and educators have enjoyed browsing it for fun crafts and activities.

Louise lives in the United Kingdom with her three children, Harry, Daisy and Ollie, and her husband, John. She has a BA (Hons) degree in Education and Art and is a qualified primary school teacher. She has been teaching young children for over 15 years.

Since she was a child, Louise has always loved art and crafts and is passionate about sharing her creative ideas, not only with her own children and the children she teaches, but also with readers all over the world.

Louise has a large social following, and her popular crafts and activities have often been featured on other websites as well as in magazines.

For more fun painting, craft or activity ideas, visit www.messylittlemonster.com or follow Messy Little Monster on Facebook (www.facebook.com/messylittlemonster) or Instagram (www.instagram.com/messylittlemonster).

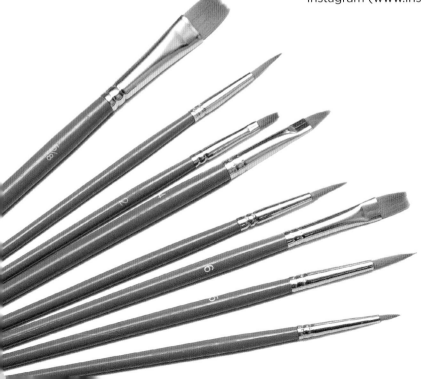

INDEX